Astrology

Sheila Geddes

An *ideals* Publication
First Printing

ISBN 0-89542-901-2 295

Consultant
Laurie Brady
Psychic Astrologer, Lecturer, Writer

Library of Congress Catalog Number: 80-80259

Copyright © MCMLXXX by Ideals Publishing Corporation
All rights reserved
Printed and bound in U.S.A.

Published by Ideals Publishing Corporation
11315 Watertown Plank Road
Milwaukee, WI 53226

First published
Macdonald Educational Ltd.
Holywell House, Worship Street,
London EC2A 2EN

Contents

Information

Activities

Reference

What is astrology?

Astrology is an ancient art that consists of the interpretation of the movements of the sun, moon, and planets. The fact that it is ancient does not, of course, make it valid; but the very persistence of the astrological tradition over thousands of years suggests that it contains much of value.

Modern astrologers would consider that it is both a science and an art — not an exact science like mathematics, but more like medicine, which calls for scientific knowledge on the part of the practitioner plus the art of being able to interpret the knowledge in a given situation.

Like medicine, astrology has a great legacy from the past. Present-day knowledge is built upon past traditions and discoveries. Modern techniques, such as the use of computers, constantly test the old beliefs to see whether they remain valid; where necessary, they update them.

How it all began

People who live very close to nature and who spend a great deal of their time out of doors become adept at interpreting nature's smallest signals. It seems likely that ancient peoples developed a "sixth sense" to interpret the movements they saw in the sky. We can imagine their sense of awe when they first saw the sun (which they worshiped as a god) being "swallowed up" by the moon at the time of an eclipse and the overwhelming relief with which they saw it reappear.

As people began to cultivate food, they would become aware of the sun's influence on the seasons and the moon's influence on the tides. At night they could sometimes see bright "wandering" stars; those, too, had their own characteristics. Perhaps the red one (now known as Mars) always seemed to grow in magnitude when there were tribal wars and bloodshed, so it became known and greatly feared as the warrior god.

Almost all the great ancient civilizations have left traces of their interest in astrology — Babylonian, Egyptian, Indian, Chinese, Mayan, Greek, Roman, and Arabian.

So, the first astronomers (those who study the heavens) became the first astrologers (those who interpret them). We do not know who the first astrologers were, but the first to record their findings were the Chaldeans.

A powerful influence

By the second century A. D., the practice of astrology in many countries had developed along similar lines. All the known planets had been interpreted in much the same way and given the status of gods. Thus, the planet that we call by the Roman name, Venus, was the goddess Aphrodite to the Greeks, Ishtar to the Assyrians, and Astarte to the Phoenicians — but all agreed that her influence was that of a powerful, sensuous woman, and that she was the goddess of beauty, luxury, and sexual attraction.

It is difficult for us to appreciate today just how much astrology was an accepted part of life and knowledge right up to and beyond

▶ *This Egyptian mummy case, dating from 2,000 B.C., shows the goddess Nut surrounded by the signs of the zodiac. The signs took their names originally from the constellations, named by the Chaldeans.*

▲ Alexander the Great believed in the validity of astrology and had his own court astrologer, as did many rulers and important people until the 17th century.

▲ Copernicus, the 16th century Polish astronomer, developed the theory that the sun is the center of our planetary system. This theory ultimately led to the decline of astrology.

the 16th century. Throughout history, kings and queens had their court astrologers, from the Roman Emperors and Alexander the Great to the Tudors in England and Frederick of Bohemia. Even some of the Popes and cardinals, such as Richelieu, consulted astrologers. Astrology was studied at universities, and the astrologer was a respected, learned man. Writers' works showed as much knowledge of astrology as they did of Latin and Greek.

The first rumblings of what was to be the great fall of astrology occurred during the 16th century when the idea of a universe in which the sun, and not the earth, was the center was broached. With the invention of the telescope by Galileo, the study of the heavens (astronomy) became the fashion. It quickly became respectable and rejected astrology completely.

The new awakening

The intellectuals who kept the spark alive were mostly people who accepted the theory that all life is one and that things on earth are a mirror of things in heaven. "As in the macrocosm, so in the microcosm." This, of course, was the ancient explanation of why astrology worked, and some thinkers saw no reason to abandon the theory simply because the old astronomical beliefs had been proved wrong.

Many people still hold this view, but there are many others who believe that emanations from the sun, moon, and planets affect us directly. In recent years, new scientific discoveries seem to reinforce this latter theory; and astrology is finding new converts as a result.

The birthchart and its uses

This illustration shows Beethoven's birthchart, as set up by a modern astrologer. The planets and signs of the zodiac are marked on the chart to represent a map of the heavens at the time of his birth.

Ludwig van Beethoven was born in Bonn on December 16, 1770. His ascendant (which is an important point of interpretation) is 14° Taurus — a sign closely associated with music. The planet Uranus so near the ascendant indicates genius.

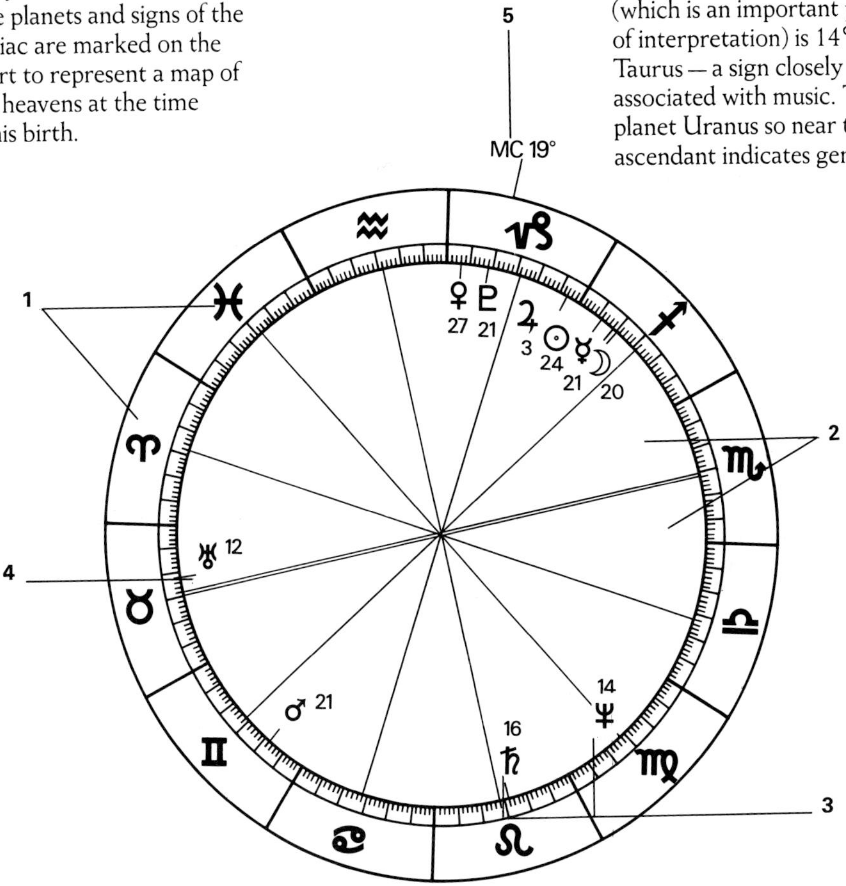

1 Signs of the zodiac.
2 These segments are called "houses."
3 Planets in the houses and signs that they occupied at the time of Beethoven's birth.
4 The ascendant: the sign and degree of the zodiac that was rising at the time of birth.
5 The MC (medium coeli) is the sign and degree that was culminating at the midheaven at the time.

The birthchart: a map of the heavens

A birthchart is a representation of the planetary system at the time and place of birth.

The top diagram is a stylized drawing of a birthchart, seen from a point above the earth at the moment of birth and showing the actual planets and the earth at the center. The observer has a kind of bird's-eye view of the whole solar system.

1 The ecliptic

The sun is shown on the circle known as the *ecliptic* in the segment known as Sagittarius. It is, of course, the earth that is moving around the sun. But just as a passenger in a moving vehicle sees stationary objects being passed as if they are moving, so it appears to us that the sun moves along a path that we call the ecliptic. The ecliptic is the central line of the zodiac.

2 The zodiac

Because the planets are moving around the sun, they also appear against a background that extends about eight degrees either side of the ecliptic and is known as the *zodiac*. For astrological purposes, this belt is divided into twelve parts of 30° each, and each part is known as a sign of the zodiac. These segments do not correspond in position to the constellations from which they take their names.

3 – 10 The planets

The small planet, Mercury (3), which can never be more than 28° from the sun, is shown nearest to the sun on the left and is also in Sagittarius. The large planet on the other side of the sun is Jupiter (4), which falls in Capricorn. Beyond Jupiter are Pluto (5) and Venus (6), which is never more than 48° from the sun. These planets are shown in Capricorn.

Diagonally opposite the sun is Mars (7), which appears against the background of Gemini. To the right of it is Uranus (8) in Taurus and farther left is the easily recognizable Saturn (9) with its rings, here shown in Leo. Slightly below it, against the background of Virgo, is the planet Neptune (10).

Although the moon (11) is much nearer to us than any of the planets, being our own satellite, it also appears to us against the background of the zodiac. In the drawing it is to the left of Mercury and in Sagittarius.

The lower diagram shows how this configuration would appear in a birthchart.

The glyph (sign) of each planet is placed in the appropriate sign of the zodiac at the exact degree that denotes its position.

Ascendant and midheaven

Two other features, normally shown on a birthchart, depend on the time of birth and the position on earth of the birthplace. These are the ascendant and midheaven. Because the earth makes one complete revolution every 24 hours, it appears to us that the whole zodiacal system revolves around us in that time. The sign that appears to be rising above the eastern horizon at the time of birth is known as the ascendant. The midheaven is the degree of the zodiac that is culminating overhead at the time and place of birth.

Cusps (12)

As the whole zodiac seems to revolve around us once in 24 hours, each of the twelve divisions takes about two hours to pass any given point on the horizon. The point at which a new sign starts is known as the cusp. When the sun moves from Sagittarius into Capricorn, for instance, it is said to be at 0° Capricorn and not 30° Sagittarius. People who are born when the sun is near a cusp often show characteristics of both signs.

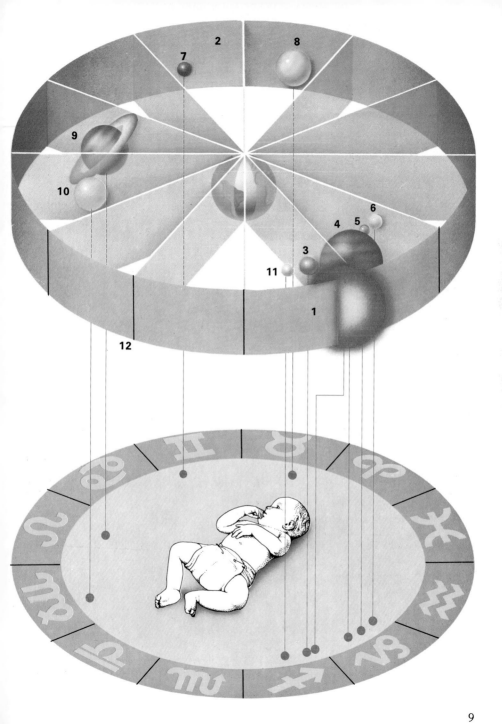

Tools of the trade

The birthchart is to an astrologer what the microscope is to a scientist. Therein lies the key to the character and potential of its subject. A *birthchart,* sometimes called a *horoscope,* is a representation of the position of the sun, moon, and planets at a given moment in time as seen from a precise spot on the earth. It can be set up — *erected* or *cast* — to represent the birth time of a person, an animal, a project, a coronation, the launching of a ship, or, indeed, anything that may be said to have a birth time.

Although astrologers are, of course, aware that the sun, moon, and planets do not move around the earth, they set up the birthchart to show the position of the lights (sun and moon) and the planets as they appear to be from the earth. To us, it appears that the sun moves through the heavens in a fixed path known as the ecliptic. The sun moves through the constellations that have given their names to the signs of the zodiac. The

planets and the moon also appear to move against this background.

The zodiac

It is very important to realize that the constellations are not the same as the signs of the zodiac. For one thing, the constellations vary greatly in size; for another, the constellation that appears to be behind the sun at the spring equinox changes gradually over the centuries, due to a slight distortion in the Earth's rotation.

For the purpose of astrology, the ecliptic is divided into twelve parts of thirty degrees each, known as the zodiac. Each part has the name of a sign of the zodiac. When the sun appears to be against the background of the part of the sky known as Taurus, it is said to be "in" Taurus, and the native (the person for whom the birthchart is set up) is said to have a Taurean sun sign.

▶ *Kepler (1571 — 1630), an astronomer and astrologer, cast this horoscope for Wallenstein and is reputed to have forecast Wallenstein's military victories. This is a good example of the square horoscope, which was used until the 20th century. Kepler believed Copernicus and eventually proved that the earth moved around the sun. Although he practiced astrology, he is quoted as saying that it was "the foolish daughter" of the "wise mother" astronomy.*

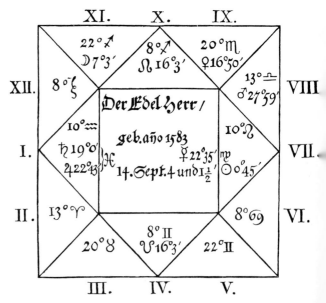

Von Keppler angeblich für Wallenstein im Jahre 1608 gestelltes Horostop

How an astrologer works

After setting up the birthchart, the astrologer has to consider the interpretation of the ascendant, the sun, the moon, and the planets, as shown by the zodiac sign in which each appears and the house it occupies.

The position of the ascendant is interpreted as showing the personality and the outward behavior. It is sometimes described as "the face presented to the world." This is in contrast to the sun sign, which is interpreted as the basic personality. The assessment of these, together with the interpretation of the moon, are the most important things to be considered. Then follow the planets, in order, due weight being given to their respective qualities.

The astrologer will then have a reasonably clear idea of the native's psychological makeup. Some planets will probably be "strong" because they are in a zodiacal sign that they are said to rule.

A further assessment is then made by working out the aspects that each planet presents to the others. By this time, the astrologer will have a mass of information about the person whose birthchart is being studied. The final task is to synthesize this so that the interpretation gives due weight to the things that are important and so that it makes sense to the native. A strong characteristic tends to be emphasized by appearing more than once within this mass of data.

▲ Greenwich meridian line. The Rev. John Flamsteed, the first Astronomer Royal, set up an electional chart to determine the date of the opening of Greenwich observatory in 1675. All degrees of longitude are reckoned from the Greenwich meridian line.

A sign of the zodiac is often said to be ruled by a planet, and a person is said to be ruled by the sign that contained the sun at the time of birth. Despite this terminology, astrologers usually state that they do not believe that the planet or zodiacal sign directly influences the native. Their explanation is that there is a correlation between the characteristics attributed to the signs and planets and the character of the native.

The uses of astrology

Personal birthcharts can be used in a variety of ways. It is often helpful to people to know their potential capabilities as revealed in the birthchart. They may not have recognized this potential, and it may therefore remain undeveloped. An adult looking for a change of career may find it helpful to be told that he

11

or she could make a success of something that had not been thought of but, when suggested, will have immediate appeal.

Another use of the personal horoscope is to compare it with that of another person with whom the native is in partnership, whether in business or emotionally. Such a comparison (known as synastry) should reveal whether they are suited to that particular partnership, where the difficulties are likely to lie, and where they can be of help to each other.

A small business firm may be considering taking on another partner. A comparison of that native's birthchart with the charts of the existing partners may show that person a welcome addition. Astrologers are now actually employed by businesses that require this kind of service.

The interpretation of a child's birthchart can be of great help to the parents in indicating the kind of upbringing this particular child requires, the type of school, and the ultimate career that will be most suitable.

Astrologers who deal with this type of personal astrology are used to dealing with all kinds of problems at a psychological level, including health and marital problems. The ability to interpret future trends often means that the astrologer can give a person who is in some difficulty a fairly good idea of when this trend is likely to pass.

Different types of astrology

It is possible to choose a birth time for a project which is in the future. This is known as "electional" astrology. In the Far East it has always been used for choosing a marriage date at a time when the planetary pattern is propitious; it is now becoming more widely used in the western world. Nowadays, it is fairly common for an astrologer to be asked to supply several dates that would be suitable

for the opening of a new business or society. On a personal level, a client may ask when a new venture would best be undertaken.

Most astrologers will assess the future trends in the lives of their clients. But it is often difficult to pinpoint precisely the times when certain things might occur; and many astrologers do not like attempting future forecasts in detail. However, clients can certainly expect to be told the times when they have maximum opportunities and the times when it would pay them to "play it cool."

As they did in the heyday of astrology, astrologers are once again working closely with doctors (of all types). Those who use astrological data to assess their patients' conditions and to discover when they are most at risk are becoming increasingly convinced of the validity of such data. Carl Jung, the great Swiss psychologist, was one of the first to use astrology as a guide to the psychological makeup of his patients.

Political forecasting

There are also astrologers who deal with political events. This practice is known as "mundane" astrology. Such astrologers are able to assess political and economic trends. To do this, they study the birthchart of the country and the charts of significant political figures.

Finally, many astrologers are currently engaged in scientific work, such as weather forecasting and the investigation of planetary cycles. This latter work has already produced some useful results. It is interesting that this is one of the ways in which astrology has been generally accepted, although the professional meteorologists, who study planetary cycles to judge their effect on our weather, would probably deny that they practice astrology.

Once again, astrology is alive and well all over the world and shows every sign of continuing to grow and to be widely used in the future.

◀ *The scene in Dallas, seconds before President Kennedy's assassination in November 1963. The American astrologer, Leslie McIntyre, had written six months previously that there would be "personal danger to our head of state" at that time. Astrologers were aware that his birthchart indicated danger from explosives.*

▶ *This hieroglyph shows another successful forecast by an astrologer. In 1651, William Lilly predicted the Great Fire of London, which occurred fifteen years later in 1666. It shows Gemini (the twins) — the sign that rules London — falling into flames. Lilly was at first suspected of starting the fire to make his prediction come true!*

Lights and planets

The sun

As the sun is the life-giving force to the earth, so it is interpreted, astrologically, as the creative principle. It is usually the dominating feature of the birthchart, and the zodiacal sign it occupies will show the type of personality and the mode of self-expression of the native. Most people will show many, if not all, of the characteristics of their sun sign.

Physically, the sun rules the heart (being the heart of our solar system) and the spine. Astrologically, it is the ruler of Leo and is considered to be a "masculine" planet, embodying the principle of fatherhood and authority. The sign for the sun represents the complete whole (the circle) with the life seed inside it and is similar to the cells in the human body.

▼ *An Egyptian relief showing Akhenaten and Nefertiti worshipping the sun. The ancient Egyptians believed that a boat ferried the sun across the sky from east to west every day.*

Mrs. Margaret Hone, former Principal of the Faculty of Astrological Studies, devised some keywords to describe each of the planets and zodiacal signs. These proved to be so useful as an aide-memoire for the interpretation that we have introduced similar keywords here.

The sun
Keywords: regal, dignified, powerful, creative, dramatic, generous, loving, lively. See also words that relate to Leo, the sign ruled by the sun.

The moon

Because the moon is a satellite of the earth and is much nearer to us than any of the planets, we are aware that it has a direct effect on life on earth. In particular, we know that it is responsible for the ebb and flow of the tides. Science has now established that the moon exerts its pull on all water; since water is the largest constituent of the human body, it appears that the moon's movement directly influences us.

The moon's position in a birthchart shows the native's response to life, his or her subconscious reactions, and the basic impulses. It is a very important factor in a birthchart. In certain circumstances, the moon's sign characteristics will be stronger than those of the sun sign. First impressions of a person are likely to give a clue to the moon's position in the birthchart.

Psychologically, the moon's position is particularly significant. It often affects decisions made at an early age due to conditions in the home and the characters of the parents. These decisions are sometimes carried into adult life, even though they are no longer appropriate. A good astrologer will help a client to reexamine them to see whether they are still valid.

Because the moon influences the growth of plant life on earth, it is associated with fertility. Astrologically, it rules the sign of Cancer, which indicates the maternal instinct. Physically, it relates to the breasts, stomach, and digestive system.

▼ *These pictures show the island of Mount St. Michael with the tide in and out. The moon has the greatest influence on our tides; but, at new and full moon, the sun and moon work together to produce strong, spring tides.*

The moon ☽
Keywords: responsive, home-loving, imaginative, sensitive, receptive, changeable, moody. See also words relating to Cancer.

Mercury

The mythological Mercury was known as the Messenger of the Gods. Astrologically, this planet rules communication — speech, writing, travel. Its position in the birthchart indicates the type of mentality of the native and the nervous system. The nerves are messengers that carry communications to and from the brain.

Physically, Mercury rules the nervous system, lungs, brain, and thyroid. In the interpretation of a child's birthchart, the astrologer would consider the position of Mercury (that is, the zodiacal sign and the house it was in) to discover what type of education would be beneficial.

Astrologically, it rules the signs Gemini and Virgo. The symbol for Mercury is the half-circle (representing human spirit or mind) over the circle (divine spirit — the complete whole) and the cross (earthly

◀ *The prehistoric stone circle at Stonehenge in England, built about 1900 B.C., is thought to have been used to study the heavens. It may have been used to predict eclipses and to measure the time of the summer and winter solstices.*

▶ *This 16th century German woodcut depicts the various activities that the planet Mercury is said to rule. These include teaching, writing, debating, learning, and public speaking — all of a mental and communicative nature. The influence of astrology was very wide at the time, and woodcuts such as these were used in the teaching of the subject.*

matter) below both. Until you are familiar with all the signs, it may be easier to remember it as the sign for the planet Venus, with the addition of the wings of Mercury's winged helmet. The common name for mercury — quick-silver — suggests speed and movement.

luxuries of life is a very Venusian trait.

Physically, Venus rules the throat, kidneys, and parathyroids. Astrologically, it rules Taurus and Libra.

The sign for Venus is the symbol used in medicine and biology to denote "female."

Mercury
Keywords: adept, clever, cool-natured, expressive, intelligent, critical, perceptive. See also words relating to Gemini and Virgo.

Venus ♀
Keywords: artistic, companionable, graceful, peace-loving, friendly, beauty-loving, sensuous. See also words relating to Taurus and Libra.

Venus

Astronomically, Venus is the nearest to earth of the inferior planets, the ones between the sun and the earth. We can see it very clearly with the naked eye; it is a most beautiful morning star when its orbit brings it close to us. It is no wonder, then, that the ancients thought of it as having the influence of a beautiful woman.

As one might expect of the goddess of love, the position of Venus in the birthchart indicates the type of personal relationships the native can make. In contrast to Mercury, it is the feelings, rather than the mentality, that dominate the Venusian personality. The love in this sense is not only strongly erotic, but also signifies the need for warmth and affection and the desire to return them. Venus was also known as the goddess of beauty, and the love of beauty in all its forms is indicated by the planet's position (by zodiacal sign and house). Desire for the possession of beautiful things and for the

Mars

Mars is our nearest neighbor on the side farther from the sun (the first of the superior planets). It appears to us as a red disc and is consequently known as the red planet.

Mars was the Roman god of war, and the old astrologers considered that Mars indicated violence and quick temper. Present-day astrologers regard it more as indicating the degree of initiative and energy in the makeup of the subject of a birthchart. It is certainly a very potent planet, signifying pioneering instincts, passion in all its forms, health, and leadership

▶ *This mosaic from Pompeii depicts Venus, acclaimed since ancient times as the goddess of beauty and love. She appears in the mythology of many different civilizations under various names.*

An astrologer would look at the position of Mars together with that of the sun, in order to judge the health and vitality of the native.

Physically, it rules the sex glands, the muscular and uro-genital systems, and the adrenal glands. Astrologically, it rules the sign Aries.

The sign for Mars is the symbol used in medicine and biology for "male." The arrowhead expresses the forcefulness and drive of this planet.

Mars
Keywords: energetic, forceful, pioneering, impulsive, passionate, direct, decisive. Other related words will be found under Aries.

Jupiter

In his *Planets Suite,* Holst describes Jupiter, or Jove, as the bringer of jollity. In astrology, this planet is considered to be the great benefactor, the bestower of good. It signifies cheerfulness, or joviality. The position of Jupiter in the birthchart shows the way in which the native seeks pleasures or expansion.

Perhaps more than any of the planets we have mentioned so far, Jupiter's influence seems to have a spiritual significance, although the whole birthchart can be interpreted on that level. An expansion of consciousness, aspirations, and a philosophical outlook are all associated with Jupiter, who was, of course, the father of the gods. On a more mundane level, material expansion and growth are achieved as plans mature; maturity is also attributed to Jupiter.

Physically, this planet rules the liver and pituitary gland. Astrologically, it rules the sign Sagittarius. The sign for Jupiter is a half circle at right angles to a cross.

Jupiter 2+
Keywords: fortunate, generous, expansive, aspiring, philosophical, broad-minded, optimistic, mature. See also words that relate to Sagittarius.

◀ *This representation of Mars, from an Italian manuscript, shows him as the god of war. Note the soldiers. A contemporary French statistician, Prof. Michel Gauquelin, has found the planet Mars prominent in the birthcharts of famous soldiers.*

Saturn

Saturn is the "cold" planet, causing limitation and frustration and imposing discipline on the native, often by means of added responsibilities. We say that life teaches us, and Saturn appears to be the great teacher. Its lessons are often hard, but without them we should not achieve anything.

▼ *This woodcut represents the astrological characteristics attributed to Jupiter: philosophy, law, and authority.*

▶ *The planet Saturn, which was thought to be the most distant planet of our solar system until Uranus was discovered in 1781.*

This planet is said to represent the father in the birthchart. It may help you to remember Saturn's role if you think of the image of the Victorian father, the strict disciplinarian for the good of the child.

Physically, Saturn rules the skin and bones, the teeth and gall bladder. Astrologically, it rules the sign of Capricorn.

The sign for Saturn has been described as being reminiscent of Father Time's sickle.

♄

Saturn
Keywords: practical, ambitious, patient, reliable, disciplinary, responsible, controlled, just. Other related words will be found under Capricorn.

---

of three that were discovered in comparatively modern times. Herschel identified it in 1781. It was originally called by his name and still appears as Herschel in some books.

Uranus was discovered at a time of change and revolution. Nations were being formed or were breaking away from old dominations; above all, people were seeking freedom and were banding together to achieve it. The position of Uranus in the birthchart gives an indication of the native's ability to make changes, including disruptive and revolutionary ones, to act impulsively and unconventionally, and to seek personal freedom.

Physically, Uranus rules the circulatory system and, probably, the pineal gland. Astrologically, it rules the sign of Aquarius.

The sign for Uranus shows an H for Herschel; the complete sign is like the old type of television aerial. Television being a new, scientific invention, is associated with Uranus.

Uranus

The planets already described were known to the ancient astrologers; Uranus is the first

▶ *San Francisco after the earthquake of 1906. Rudolf Tomaschek, a German geophysicist, has discovered that Uranus was culminating at the time of large earthquakes.*

22

Neptune

Holst called this planet "the mystic," and most astrologers would agree. When Neptune was discovered, in 1846, people were starting to experiment with practices they considered mystic, such as mesmerism and hypnotism, and the Spiritualist movement had just started. In the old mythology, Neptune was the god of the sea, in itself the great unknown element, which was often described as boundless. The planet seems to correlate with the need to escape from all that confines or limits the native. In the birthchart, the position of Neptune shows the ways the intuition or inspiration will be used.

Physically, this planet rules the thalamus, the spinal canal, and the mental and nervous

systems. Astrologically, it rules the sign of Pisces.

The sign for Neptune may be remembered by its likeness to the trident of the sea god.

Pluto

This planet was discovered in 1930. Pluto was the god of the underworld in mythology. Although we have had little time, scientifically speaking, to observe its effects, the planet appears to correlate with the unknown — death and life beyond death. Psychologically, it refers to the unconscious. The position of Pluto in the birthchart shows the extent to which the hidden forces in the subconscious can be brought out by the native to be either used or discarded.

Physically, Pluto rules the reproductive system. Astrologically, it rules the sign of Scorpio.

The sign for Pluto is a combination of the initials of Percival Lowell, who did the work that led to its discovery.

Signs of the zodiac

The ancient astrologers peopled the heavens with animals, gods, and heroes, much as children see cloud pictures. The twelve constellations that lie on the ecliptic have given their names to the signs of the zodiac.

Positive and negative signs

No one sign is better than another. Each holds within it the potential for good or evil, and qualities that are admirable if used rightly can become faults through misuse or overstress.

As well as its individual characteristics, each sign is said to be either positive or negative. Positive signs describe a tendency to be extroverted and negative signs, a tendency to be introverted.

The zodiacal signs also fall into categories according to the elements that rule them. These elements are fire, earth, air, and water. The fire and air signs are all positive; the earth and water signs are all negative.

The elements, or triplicities

These elements are called the *triplicities;* each category contains three signs. Fire signs are Aries, Leo, and Sagittarius. The nature of fire is to be energetic, enthusiastic, and positive. Earth signs are Taurus, Virgo, and Capricorn. The nature of earth is to be practical, static, and negative. Air signs are Gemini, Libra and Aquarius. The nature of air is to be communicative, intellectual, and positive. Water signs are Cancer, Scorpio, and Pisces. The nature of water is to be impressionable, emotional, and negative.

The qualities, or quadruplicities

There is a further category, known as the *quadruplicities* in which each group contains four signs. The qualities are *cardinal, fixed* or *mutable.* Cardinal signs are Aries, Cancer, Libra, and Capricorn. The quality of the cardinal signs is to be active. Fixed signs are Taurus, Leo, Scorpio, and Aquarius. The quality of fixed signs is to be cautious. Mutable signs are Gemini, Virgo, Sagittarius, and Pisces. The quality of the mutable signs is to be adaptable.

The mutable signs are often referred to as the common signs, but the word *mutable* is used throughout this book to express the quality of adaptability.

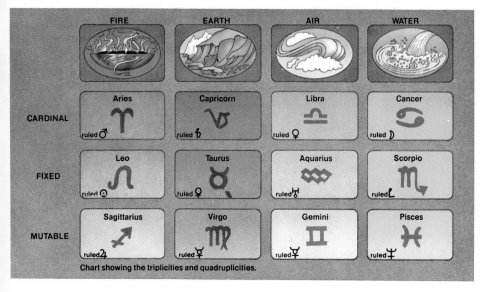

Chart showing the triplicities and quadruplicities.

The names of the signs

The ancient Chaldeans, who named most of the signs of the zodiac, believed that the sun traveled around the earth. Its apparent path, known as the ecliptic, passed through twelve constellations, so at a certain time the sun could be said to be "in" each constellation. Because the earth takes slightly more than a year to travel around the sun, the signs of the zodiac no longer coincide with the constellations from which they took their names. 0° Aries is now in the constellation of Pisces. The modern zodiac divides the signs equally into twelve segments of 30° each.

The names themselves were invented to describe the patterns formed by the stars. Some of the names are difficult to justify, and one feels that ancient astrologers and astronomers must have had vivid imaginations!

In Gemini, here shown with the twins superimposed, it is likely that the name originated from the two bright stars, Castor and Pollux, in the constellation.

The diagram shows the southern hemishpere on the left and the northern hemisphere on the right.

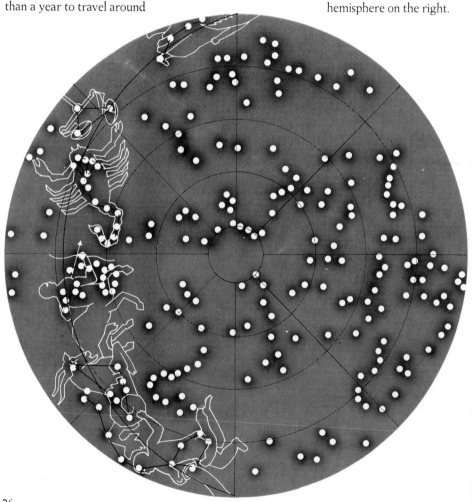

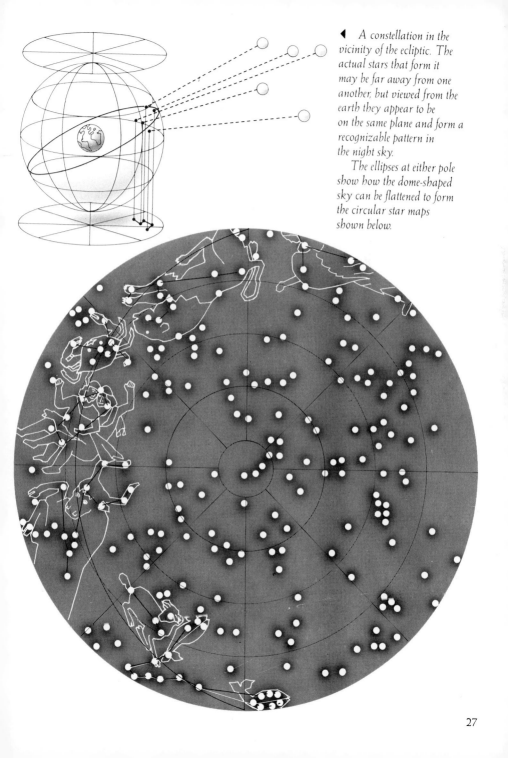

◀ *A constellation in the vicinity of the ecliptic. The actual stars that form it may be far away from one another, but viewed from the earth they appear to be on the same plane and form a recognizable pattern in the night sky.*

The ellipses at either pole show how the dome-shaped sky can be flattened to form the circular star maps shown below.

▾ *Aries, the Ram, is here depicted jumping through the circle of the sun's path, signifying the spring equinox.*

▶ *This fine bull's head from Crete recalls the legend of Europa who was taken there by the god, Jupiter, disguised as a bull. The dangerous sport of bull-leaping flourished in Crete and is depicted in much of its art.*

The spring equinox begins when the sun enters the sign of Aries on about the 22nd of March each year. The sun enters a zodiacal sign between the 20th and 23rd of each month, depending on the year. The dates given are, therefore, approximate.

Aries (The Ram)

The sun is in this sign from March 21 to April 19. Aries is of the fire triplicity and the cardinal quadruplicity. The nature of fire is to be energetic, enthusiastic, and positive; the cardinal quality is to be active. So the Arian is all of these things. As Aries is ruled by Mars, all the Martian attributes are also emphasized: energy, initiative, and qualities of leadership.

Aries people are self-oriented, and their considerable energies are used in pursuit of their own goals. Quickness and impulsiveness are typical. The head is the part of the body that correlates with Aries, and the expressions "head first" and "headstrong" might have been coined to describe a typical Arian. The Aries person's bravery and disregard for danger is legendary. Indeed, dangerous situations have great appeal, as they call for quick action, initiative, leadership, and courage.

The Arian has a strong pioneering spirit and loves to start new things, but loses interest when they become mundane. He or she can be pugnacious and quick-tempered, but will as quickly recover; words such as patience and tact are not in the Arian's vocabulary. You are likely to get some scorching home truths from an Arian — he or she is too direct to be subtle. The Arian is

quick-witted, but not always logical, good at making quick decisions, and performs well under pressure. Arians will study energetically if the subject appeals to them but not otherwise. They can be rather childish if they fail to get their own way, but the sheer life and exuberance in their natures makes them stimulating companions. The Arian's sexual nature is strong and positive, but not to the exclusion of romance.

Suitable careers will be found among the jobs that require energy and initiative. The Arian likes challenges and to be in charge of a project. Arians do well as explorers, pioneers, surgeons, soldiers, professional sportsmen, racing drivers, engineers, and in related professions. They also make good psychologists and psychiatrists.

The above description will apply to a person who has sun, moon, or ascendant in Aries; also to someone with Mars in Aries. Mars is then said to be "strong in its own sign."

> ♈
>
> **Aries**
> **Keywords: impulse, anger, courage, energy, sharpness, leadership, wit, redness, iron, acid, and all Martian words.**

Taurus (The Bull)

The sun is in this sign from April 20 to May 20. Taurus is of the earth triplicity and the fixed quadruplicity. The nature of earth is to be practical, static, and negative;

▼ *In this Roman relief, Mithras, the Persian god, is shown slaying the sacred bull as a sacrifice to the sun god. Mithraism later became popular in Rome and was the chief rival of Christianity until the time of Constantine.*

▲ *This representation of the Gemini (twins) comes from a Persian manuscript of about A.D. 1650.*

and the fixed quality is to be cautious. The ruling planet, Venus, contributes the principles of harmony and relatedness.

The Taurean native is practical and reliable, patient, and determined. This latter quality easily becomes obstinacy and resistance to change. The Taurean needs the feeling of security and, in order to ensure it, tends to be acquisitive and possessive. Taureans often have a flair for handling money and interest in the worlds of finance and big business. They are not afraid of responsibility.

The Venusian influence makes Taureans connoisseurs of the good things in life, susceptible to beauty in all its forms, and well aware of the merit — and, therefore, the value — of works of art. Their tempers are not quickly aroused, but can be frightening when they have been. "Bull in a china shop" is a good phrase to describe the Taurean at such times. The Taurean is usually a nature-lover, often a gardener, and a lover of comforts:

food, wine, and a comfortable home, which will be as luxurious as he or she can make it. This native has a true down-to-earth attitude and likes to put his or her money into land or real estate.

Taureans are not quick-witted, and they do not enjoy debate; having made up their minds, they are not likely to change them. They do not learn quickly, but they learn thoroughly. They are methodical and deliberate and so predictable that they can become boring.

Emotionally, they need happy and stable relationships. They are warm-natured, very affectionate and sensual, appreciating the body and its pleasures. Possessiveness is their great fault and jealousy the most likely result.

Suitable careers will be found in natural surroundings as a farmer, gardener, florist, or horticulturist; in artistic work and music; in financial fields as stockbroker, treasurer, banker, accountant, economist; or as an architect or builder. This description will apply to anyone who has sun, moon, ascendant, or Venus in Taurus.

Taurus
Keywords: art, possessions, money, property, land, beauty, music, singing, gardens, affection, sensuousness, and all Venusian words.

Gemini (The Twins)

The sun is in this sign from May 21 to June 21. Here we have a combination of the air element with the mutable quality. The nature of air is to be communicative, intellectual,

The constellation of Gemini, the twins, has been known from the earliest times. It probably took its name from Castor and Pollux, the two brightest stars in the constellation.

This woodcut shows the activities of the months of mid-May to mid-July (ruled by Gemini and Cancer) in the country year.

and positive; and the mutable quality is to be adaptable. Gemini is ruled by Mercury, which represents communication and mentality. People who have Gemini strong in their birthchart are mentally-oriented, intelligent, adaptable, and quick in mind and movement.

Thoughts and words are the things that matter to Geminis, and they use them all the time. Quick and lively in debate, Geminis can easily become devil's advocates, since they change their minds often. This quality (the sign of the twins), shows itself in many ways. Geminis will often have two, or more, projects on the fire, two love affairs, even two careers. They need plenty of variety and will stagnate in the routine conditions Taureans would enjoy. Their restlessness pays dividends in the kind of career that requires travel and allows them to plan their own hours of work. However, activity often becomes movement for its own sake, with no end product, and learning becomes superficial, so that the Gemini ends up by knowing a little about a multitude of things, and has no deep knowledge of anything.

Geminis are rather cold and may give an impression of standoffishness, although

This panel from St. Mary's Church, Shrewsbury depicts Cancer, the crab, although it seems unlikely that the artist had ever seen a crab. Astrological symbols often appeared in churches.

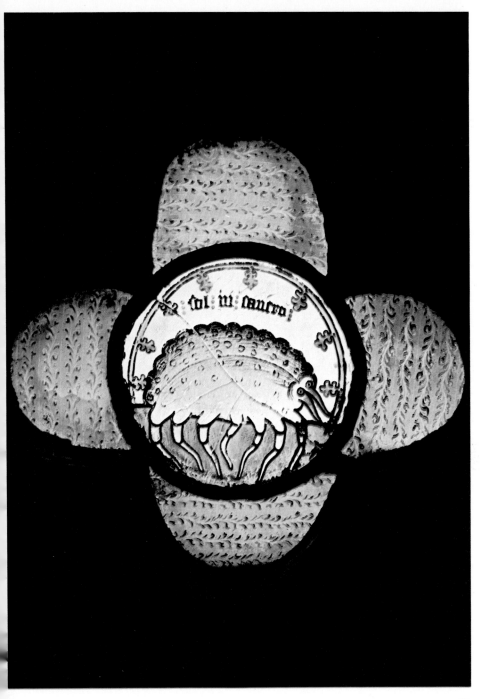

they like to flirt in a lighthearted way. Because of their need for communication, they form good relationships with others, especially where there are common interests. They tend to remain close to their families all through life, particularly to their brothers and sisters.

Suitable careers will be found in communications of all kinds, e.g., journalist, author, dramatist, news reporter, telephonist, teacher, lecturer, linguist; in travel, courier, travel agent, chauffeur, and commercial traveler.

The above description will apply substantially to those who have sun, moon, ascendant, or Mercury in Gemini.

♊

Gemini
Keywords: letters, books, stories, reports, radio, telephone, roads, railways, twins, dexterity, handicrafts, and all Mercurial words.

Cancer (The Crab)

The sun is in this sign from June 22 to July 22. The mixture for Cancer is water element and cardinal quality. The nature of water is to be emotional, intuitive, and negative. The cardinal quality is to be active. The ruler of Cancer is the moon, which expresses basic impulses and responses. The maternal nature is represented by this sign. Active in her role of mother, the female Cancerian is bound by emotional ties to her children, responsive to their needs, and feels intuitively what they require of her.

Cancerian men feel protective toward their own pet projects and enjoy doing jobs

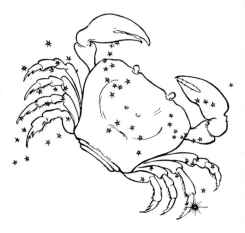

▲ *The Chaldeans believed that Cancer was "the gate of men" through which souls descended to earth as newborn babies. Astrologers interpret it as the maternal sign of the zodiac.*

in which they are looking after others, as well as their own families. Cancerians whose babies are threatened behave like a tigress with her young or the crab with its claws at the ready: fiercely protective and tenacious.

As the moon's influence causes the ebb and flow of the tides, so the Cancerian swings from one mood to another. Sensitivity and sympathy become hypersensitivity and self pity; kindness becomes irritability, and children must behave until the parent is in a good mood again.

Cancerians are good homemakers. They love their families despite their faults and will brook no criticism of them from an outsider. They appear to be tough and self-assured but are actually sensitive and easily hurt; their ready sympathy makes them suckers for a hard luck story. They have good memories, intuition, and imagination. They tend to be unoriginal in their opinions and to adopt other people's ideas. They are great worriers and even feel guilty if they cannot find anything to worry about!

Cancerians look for partners who will make good parents. They will make a comfortable home. But, although they are romantic and warm, they are primarily concerned with the children, and the partner may take second place or, more likely, be treated as one of the children.

Suitable careers will be found in jobs connected with looking after people, e.g., caterers, hoteliers, nurses, or domestic-science teachers; in jobs connected with the sea, e.g., fishermen, or sailors; and in jobs to do with the past, e.g., antique dealers, auctioneers,

historians, and curators.

The above description will apply substantially to all who have sun, moon, or ascendant in Cancer.

Cancer
Keywords: memory, home, antiquity, food, motherhood, tides, and all moon words.

▼ *Leo is among the most ancient of the constellations. Like modern astrologers, early Babylonians and Indians associated Leo with the sun. It was worshiped by the Egyptians and it is thought that the sphinx may be a representation of it.*

Leo (The Lion)

The sun is in this sign from July 23 to August 22. The fire element with the fixed quality seems like a contradiction, since fire is

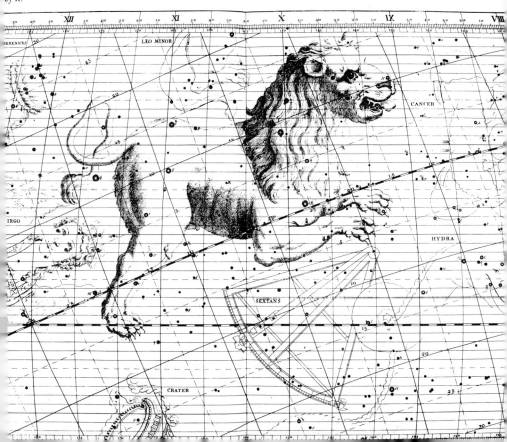

energetic, enthusiastic, and positive while fixity is cautious. Leos have enough practicality to harness their enthusiasm and turn it to good use. The sun is the ruler, bringing vitality and revealing the true self. Leo is both king of the forest and the sun god.

Leo natives instinctively feel that their place is at the top and act accordingly. So powerful is this attitude that others accept them at their own valuation and frequently put them into management positions. One could say of Leo natives that they are both born great and have greatness thrust upon them. They are natural leaders (like the other fire sign, Aries) but with the practicality of the fixed quality, which also makes them good organizers.

Sunny by nature, the Leo is warmhearted, generous, and magnanimous and so has lots of friends. Leo natives tend to be larger than life and always do things in a big way. This can develop into an arrogant and domineering attitude, if not corrected in early life. Only the best is good enough for them, and they can be wildly extravagant.

▲ *This representation of Leo's month (August) from a French book of the 15th century gives some idea of the great influence of astrology at that time.*

Leo people's feelings of pride and self-respect give them an innate dignity. They are consummate actors, and this dignity makes them put on a mask of well-being when things are against them. When things get tough, Leos show the courage of the lion, not, as Aries would, by going out to fight (cardinal), but by refusing to be moved (fixed).

Leos have the conservatism of their fixity. Opinions, once formed, are held forever. However, their thinking is constructive and, once committed to a course, they will see it through. Leos ideas will be on a large scale (without too much attention to detail) and with a breadth of vision that again shows their courage; they are not afraid of tackling anything because of its size.

Leos have the sexuality associated with all the fire signs, combined with genuine and warm affection. They can be easily hurt, but will hide the fact. Because Leo natives set high standards for themselves they are quickly disappointed when others fall short or when they feel that they are not sufficiently appreciated.

Suitable careers are found among those that call for leadership as managing directors, public relations officers, professional sportspersons, actor-managers, producers, impressarios, film stars; also as goldsmiths and jewelers.

The above description will apply substantially to those with sun, moon, or ascendant in Leo.

Leo   ♌

Keywords: kingship, fatherhood, jewels, gold, regal, warmth, fire, sunshine, drama, happiness, command, courage, size, creation, breadth, and all sun words.

Virgo (The Virgin)

The sun is in this sign from August 23 to September 22. The earth element is combined with the mutable quality, giving a mix of practical, static, and negative with adaptability, plus the nature of the ruler, Mercury, adding communications and mentality factors.

The practicality of earth gives Virgo the means to use Mercury's gifts in material ways. Office routine will be acceptable, so the mind will be used in business occupations and in ways that produce tangible results in the form of an end product. Virgos have a great facility for critical and detailed work. The mind wants to know how things work, and Virgos will go to great lengths to find

▼ *In Egyptian mythology, the goddess Isis, escaping from Typhon, dropped her corn sheaf. She became Virgo and the scattered corn became the Milky Way.*

out. The connection with the image of virginity is shown in a desire for purity, for wholesomeness of food, for cleanliness to the point of fussiness, and a great interest in health, hygiene, and diet.

The desire to serve other people is very important to Virgos, but they prefer to work in the background, being too shy to be happy in the limelight and lacking self-confidence. The precision and attention to detail that is second nature to the Virgo easily becomes fault-finding fussiness that can be irritating to others. This preciseness, combined with a lot of nervous energy, enables the Virgo to put in a more than adequate day's work. Virgos are the hardest workers in the zodiac. They have shrewd, analytical minds, capable of

▼ *This woodcut shows the activities of September in the pastoral year and depicts Virgo and Libra, the signs that share the month astrologically.*

precision work and have the ability to assess critically. Obsession with details sometimes means that the Virgo "can't see the forest for the trees" and loses sight of the main object.

The virginal attitude can result in a touch-me-not air, but the Virgo's true kindness and desire to help people means that he or she is not short of appreciative friends. Sexual feelings are not strong, and there may be difficulty if the Virgo has a demanding partner. This will be mitigated if Venus and Mars are in fire signs.

Suitable careers will be found in communications as teacher, lecturer, or drama critic; in business, as secretary or civil servant; in health, as dietician, naturopath, or public health officer; in precision work, as analyst or statistician. There is also a high degree of manual dexterity, and careers as craftspersons of all types will appeal.

The above description will apply substantially to those with sun, moon, ascendant or Mercury in Virgo.

Virgo ♍
Keywords: work, diet, natural, harvest, corn, animals, health, teaching, precision, analysis, handiwork, details, criticism, and all Mercurian words.

Polarity

Half the signs of the zodiac have now been described. Each of the signs that follow will balance its opposite number, being in opposition to it as the North Pole is to the South Pole. These opposing signs are said to be in *polarity*. The first six signs represent people who, by and large, operate in their own small spheres. Those that follow are more concerned with relationships with others and tend to act in a wider context.

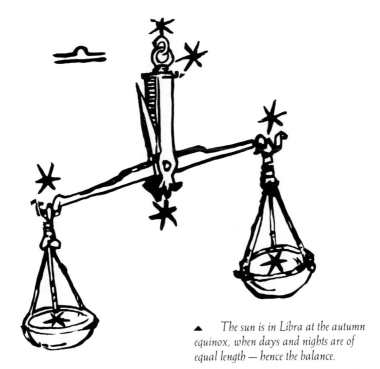

▲ *The sun is in Libra at the autumn equinox, when days and nights are of equal length — hence the balance.*

Libra (The Scales)

The sun is in this sign from September 23 to October 23. The air element is combined here with the cardinal quality, so we have a mixture of communicative, intellectual, and positive elements with an active quality and the rulership of Venus representing harmony and relationship. The Librans with the air element prominent, feel a need to communicate with their partners. They seek a balanced relationship.

As Libra is the sign of the scales, or the balance, the feeling for justice is strong in the native. "It's not fair" is a constant cry; the Libran often seems unable to accept the fact that life is not fair and becomes very resentful of any bad luck.

Librans who avoid this discontented attitude are usually charming people. They do not quarrel themselves and, in characteristically diplomatic fashion, they try to reunite those who do. Like the Taureans, they enjoy the good things of life, such as beauty, relaxation, good food, wine, and company. They can exert themselves when necessary, but they would much rather not. They enjoy entertaining and being entertained.

An ability to see both sides of a question is a very Libran trait. This ties in with the idea of balance, but does not hamper the Libran in making decisions. It seems likely that a business partnership of two Librans would be doomed to failure, for plans would never be final.

Librans are gentle people who like everything to be pleasant. They seem to be incapable of coping with ugly, dirty, or uncongenial surroundings. If they are forced to work in

such conditions, they can become nervous and even ill.

The polarity to Aries is shown by the Libran's necessity for a partner, in contrast to the Arian's self-oriented attitude.

Librans are intelligent and well able to communicate, as one would expect with an air sign. The clear thinking, that enables them to balance both sides of a problem does not, unfortunately, help them to make up their minds. For this reason, a Libran may adopt the ideas of a stronger partner rather than forming independent opinions. A Libran can do well in business, however, especially with the right partner.

Librans are so anxious to find mates that they tend to rush into love affairs. Their warm affection and desire to make life pleasant for others, and for themselves, makes them charming, thoughtful lovers or friends. They will, however, tend to expect perfection in their partners and may be too quick to weigh up their faults.

Suitable careers are to be found in all the

 An old representation of the sign of Libra; the sides of equal length again suggest balance. The Greeks regarded the constellation as part of Scorpio.

beauty and luxury trades, e.g., artist, beautician, hairdresser, antique dealer, jeweler; also in go-between situations, e.g., diplomat, receptionist, auctioneer, appraisers, legal counsel.

The above description will apply substantially to all who have sun, moon, ascendant, or Venus in Libra.

♎

Libra
Keywords: beauty, art, partnership, tact, charm, relaxation, affection, compromise, diplomacy, laziness, and all Venusian words.

40

Parts of the body ruled by signs of the zodiac

The idea that the different signs of the zodiac (and planets) rule different parts of the body belongs to the old traditional astrology.

Hippocrates (460-377 B.C.), often called "the father of medicine," declared that a physician who did not understand astrology had no right to call himself a physician. Modern astrologers recognize the validity of many of the old beliefs.

Aries
Head

Taurus
Throat

Gemini
Lungs, arms

Leo
Heart, back

Cancer
Breasts, stomach

Libra
Kidneys, lumbar region

Virgo
Nervous system, intestines

Sagittarius
Liver, hips, thighs

Scorpio
Sexual organs

Pisces
Feet, pituitary gland

Aquarius
Ankles, calves, circulation

Capricorn
Skin, bones

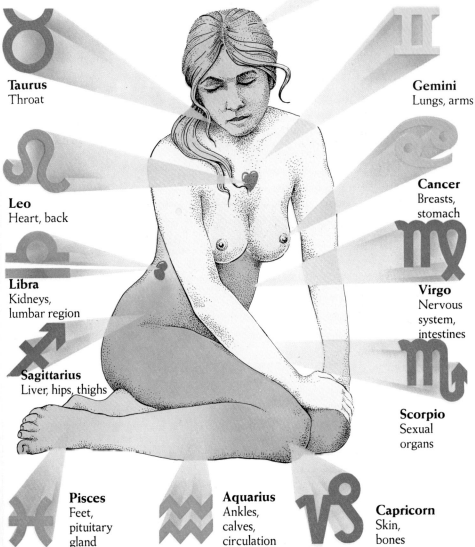

41

Scorpio (The Scorpion and Eagle)

The sun is in this sign from October 24 to November 21. In Scorpio, the water triplicity is combined with the fixed quadruplicity, so we have the emotional, intuitive, and negative element combined with a cautious quality. The emotion is channeled into practical uses.

The rulership of this sign is now attributed to Pluto, expressing regeneration and refinement. The native shows an urge to throw out obstructions and make way for new life. This is like a constant process of refining — being tried in the fire of intensity and emerging regenerated.

It has become an astrological cliché to refer to Scorpio as the most sexually passionate of the zodiacal types. In fact, the passion applies to everything that Scorpios do: work, play, embracing causes, study, etc. Everything is done and felt intensely. The double sign of the scorpion and the eagle is interestingly descriptive, since the passion can work both ways, resulting in the criminal and violent type (the scorpion with the sting) or a person with very high ideals and aspirations (the eagle, winging his way to the stars).

All the signs have characteristics that can be used for good or ill, and all can be interpreted on a spiritual level. Scorpio traits have sometimes been described as though Scorpio were the worst sign of the zodiac. Nothing could be further from the truth.

Aspiring Scorpio natives direct their passion and intensity toward good work, pouring effort into the causes they feel to be worthwhile. Because the intensity is so powerful, it follows that these traits will do much harm if ill-directed. In such cases, violence and revenge — savage and uncontrollable — may burst forth and destroy, even causing death in extreme cases.

It may be inferred from this that Scorpios are more conscious of the war in their own natures than are most people. Perhaps they are ashamed of their intense feelings and it is for this reason that they tend to be secretive.

A Scorpio may be driving forcefully towards a certain goal, but his or her friends may be completely unaware of this drive until the goal has been achieved. More likely, it is their intuitive sense, a feeling that their reasons are unfathomable to other people, that makes Scorpios keep quiet about them. Scorpios are capable, in a truly Plutonian fashion, of completely and suddenly changing their life styles for reasons that seem good to them, but would be incomprehensible to

▼ *Plague and sickness were rife in Egypt when the sun was in Scorpio, and this is believed to be the origin of the name. The constellation contains the bright star Antares.*

▲ *A zodiac wood engraving from 16th century France, showing the activities of the months. Astrology was then at the height of its influence.*

most people. Perhaps it is because of this that Scorpios tend to be secretive about their affairs.

Scorpios have penetrating minds and are able to analyze problems, but they tend to solve them by intuition, usually with success. The sharpness of the mind results in tendency toward cutting, sarcastic wit, often intended to sting, like the scorpion's tail.

The intensity needs to be released in sexual activity, but in order for this to be satisfactory the native must be genuinely in love. Scorpios' feelings are not only strong, but also deep. If feelings of resentment build up, however, they can become vindictive, jealous, and quarrelsome. The beauty and emotion of the sex act matter to Scorpios, and they will be faithful, passionate lovers. Their personal magnetism and fascination for others will ensure them plenty of willing partners; but if a Scorpio does not find the right one, the lack will be disquieting.

Suitable careers will be found in work that actively helps others, such as surgeon, spiritual healer, psychiatrist, or psychologist and in work dealing with the public welfare, such as police officer, detective, undertaker, or research worker.

The above description will apply substantially to those who have sun, moon, ascendant, or Pluto in Scorpio.

♏

Scorpio
Keywords: creation, birth, death, sex, regeneration, passion, research, secretiveness, and all Plutonian words.

Sagittarius (The Archer)

The sun is in this sign from November 22 to December 21. The mixture for Sagittarius is fire element and mutable quality, and the ruling planet is Jupiter. Thus we have energetic, enthusiastic, and positive traits combined with adaptability, expressing expansion and preservation.

The expansive nature of Sagittarians is shown in their tolerance and in the range of their minds. They take a broad view of things and are not bothered with details. This can sometimes make them seem superficial and careless.

Freedom of both mind and body is a necessity to the Sagittarian, expressing the urge to explore, both physically and mentally. They love sports, especially walking, horseback riding and all activities that use the hips and legs. Sagittarians react well to a challenge, finding it stimulating; their great enemy

▲ This fine woodcut of Sagittarius is a typical representation of the archer and horseman, often shown as a centaur.

is boredom. They are capable of deep and profound study on subjects that really interest them, but also enjoy knowing a little about a great many subjects. The Sagittarian is a philosopher and, in a spiritual sense, realizes the value of detachment from worldly cares. True to their ruler, Jupiter, Sagittarians express joviality and are perennial optimists.

Sagittarians are versatile and penetrating. When the mind is sufficiently disciplined to deal with one problem at a time, there is profound wisdom, some of which is certainly intuitive. They are capable of planning large projects, but there is a reluctance to get down to details, so that sometimes the projects remain only pipe dreams.

The polarity with Gemini is shown in this versatility and in the need to have many interests. Like the Gemini, they take a superficial interest in many things, and they share Gemini's dislike of being "tied down" to routine.

Sagittarians are ardent, as one would expect from a fire sign, but the need for freedom requires a partner who understands this and will not make them feel tied down. They seek mates whose intellect is on a par with their own and who will be stimulating.

Suitable careers can be found in professions in which the wide-ranging intellect is used, such as teacher, lawyer, priest, philosopher, or writer; in work connected with animals, especially horses; and in all forms of sports and exploration, including space travel.

The above description will apply substantially to all those who have sun, moon, ascendant, or Jupiter in Sagittarius.

Sagittarius
Keywords: travel, philosophy, religion, tolerance, walking, space, freedom, aspiration, idealist, moralist, optimist, justice, exaggeration, and all Jupiterian words.

Capricorn (The Goat)

The sun is in this sign from December 22 to January 19. The earth element is combined with the cardinal quality here, and the ruler is Saturn. The planet of limitation, responsibility, and discipline combines well with the earth element, which is practical, static, and negative; but to this is added the cardinal quality of activity. This sounds like a contradiction, but it works out very accurately in Capricorns. Their practicality and "both feet on the ground" mentality (Earth) enable them to

▼ *An illustration of the hunter from the Pastoral Calendar showing activities of the month of December. The pigs are being encouraged to root for acorns — presumably to fatten them for Christmas.*

accept discipline and responsibility readily. However, they have no intention of staying in a subordinate position, and the active quality is shown by their ambition to reach the top of their profession and by their constant, active drive in this direction.

The Saturn rulership often "puts an old head on young shoulders." Capricorns show practicality and responsibility at an early age. They have the patience to take one step at a time, as long as it is taking them in the right direction. They will not be hurried; but the activity, though hidden, is still there, for they never cease to work hard with a single aim in mind — to get on.

The inability to think and act quickly precludes the possibility of getting to the

▼ *Capricorn was known as the "gate of the gods" through which the souls of men went to heaven. Cancer, its opposite sign, was the "gate of men."*

top in some professions. When that happens, Capricorns become very disappointed and depressed. They would do well to accept their limitations in such a case and seek for happiness at a different level.

The polarity with Cancer is shown in the need for security, which to the Cancerian means home life and to the Capricorn a position of stability in the business world.

The native is similar to the Taurean, another earth sign, being a slow developer and learner; but things are learned thoroughly and retained. Capricorns can construct detailed plans and, once their minds are made up, will not easily change it. Like the Cancerians they are worriers.

Emotionally, Capricorns tend to be cool, but will be faithful to their partners, once they have committed themselves. The Capricorn male will try to be a good provider and will see this as his main role in the partnership.

▲ *The Roman Emperor Augustus believed in astrology very strongly and had his birth sign, Capricorn, the goat fish or sea goat, stamped on his coins.*

Suitable careers will be in practical, routine, or organizing work, possibly as a government official, member of the armed forces, administrator; a job in the public eye as politician, school administrator, or orator; also as an osteopath, mathematician, scientist, engineer, or builder.

The above description will apply substantially to all those who have sun, moon, ascendant, or Saturn in Capricorn.

♑

Capricorn
Keywords: aspiring,
responsible, cold, prudent,
self-contained, persevering,
methodical, plodding, modest,
exacting, and all
Saturnian words.

Aquarius (The Water-Bearer)

The sun is in this sign from January 20 to February 18. The element of air is combined with a fixed quality. The ruler is Uranus, giving the unusual combination of Uranian desire for change and personal freedom with the element, which is communicative, intellectual, and positive, and the quality of caution.

Most Aquarians are friendly people, interested in others and given to humanitarian work. The difficulty of reconciling the concept of personal freedom with justice for all is, perhaps, the key to the complexity of the Aquarian character. Where Sagittarians take their freedom without making a fuss about it, Aquarians regard it as something to fight for — one of the causes among many to which they give active support.

Aquarians like to join organizations, especially those with humanitarian aims. There they will put forward many ideas, and there will be a great deal of communication. But there is also the same detached and rather cold feeling that is present in Geminis. Feelings do not go deep, and friendliness is on the surface. The essential self is not revealed; this

47

is where the quality of caution comes in.

Aquarians are very self-sufficient and self-assured. Their advanced ideas are right; therefore everyone else is wrong. They do not mind being out of step with everyone else. The Aquarians' originality, unpredictability, and unconventionality are enhanced by a charming, though slightly distant, attitude; but they can become self-opinionated rebels, indifferent to the opinions of others.

The traditional ruler of Aquarius was Saturn and a connection can certainly be seen in the coolness and firmness — not to say, obstinancy — shown by the Aquarian. This combination of Saturn (the quality of caution) and Uranus in Aquarius has been expressed as follows: "Uranian independence and unconventionality seem completely at variance with Saturnian caution and sedateness, but, on closer examination, who is more set in his ideas and determined that no one shall deflect him from his purpose than the typical revolutionary?"

The Aquarian is original, inventive, forward-looking, rational, and intelligent. The touch-me-not attitude and the strong need for freedom make for difficulties in the formation of close relationships. But loyalty and faithfulness

can be expected, once a partnership is formed. Possessiveness will make the Aquarian feel stifled; the ideal partner will be aware of this.

Suitable careers will be those of writer, orator, lecturer, scientist, inventor, astronaut, charity worker, scientific adviser to developing countries, and so on. Television, broadcasting, astrology, astronomy, and related subjects come under the rulership of Uranus; careers in these fields would be likely to appeal. Routine, conventional, and restrictive work should be avoided.

The above description will apply substantially to those who have sun, moon, ascendant, or Uranus in Aquarius.

Aquarius
Keywords: clubs, revolutionary, waves, telepathy, eccentric, perverse, intuition, freedom, protest, reform, disruption, and all Uranian words.

◀ *An unusual depiction of Aquarius, the water bearer, from a Persian manuscript of the 17th century. The constellation has always been associated with water, probably because the sun passes through it during the rainy month of February.*

▶ *A woodcut representation of Aquarius. It was in this sign that Neptune was discovered in 1846.*

49

◀ *Greek mythology relates that Venus and Cupid changed into fishes to escape from Typhon. Minerva put the fishes into the heavens to commemorate their escape.*

▶ *This image of Pisces comes from a stained-glass window in Chartres cathedral. From earliest times Babylonians, Greeks, Syrians, and Persians all described the constellation as two fishes.*

Pisces (The Fishes)

The sun is in this sign from February 19 to March 20. Pisces combines water element with mutable quality. Neptune is the ruler, bringing intuition and nebulousness to the emotional, intuitive, and negative element and the adaptable quality. This mixture results in a very sensitive nature, susceptible to conditions both around the natives and in their own inner consciousness; and Pisceans are all feelings. They are kind and gentle, easily moved, and always anxious to help those in trouble.

Such a character naturally finds much that is distressing in the real world and must use the innate adaptability to keep everything pleasant. Pisceans will adapt themselves to the company they are in, sometimes to the extent that they appear to have no opinions of their own.

Their inner lives are real life to Pisceans, and, despite some daydreamers, many live rich and full lives by following their own intuition and channeling it in constructive ways. Like Sagittarians, they realize the value of detachment from this world.

The necessity for Pisceans to escape from all their problems is so strong as to cause some of them to resort to drink or drugs for that purpose. However, with their strong sense of intuition, many recognize the danger and react violently against it by not drinking at all and by refusing even those drugs that have been prescribed for them. This built-in sixth sense should not be ignored, as Pisceans are particularly susceptible to drug poisoning.

Their sensitivity is such that Pisceans often become subject to unknown fears and nebulous apprehensions and easily become overanxious. Self-deception is common, and so is deliberate deception of others, if it will make life easier. Channeling of this characteristic often results in the imaginative works of a poet, writer, or actor; the world of make-believe is harnessed for the enjoyment of many. The

wish to escape will, doubtless, be seen by many as sheer cowardice, but it is a much more subtle thing. Possibly, W. S. Landor described the Piscean attitude when he wrote: "I strove with none, for none was worth my strife."

The polarity with Virgo is shown in the adaptability (both mutable) and in desire to serve others. Both suffer from nervous and digestive troubles due to worrying.

Mentally, Pisceans are very intuitive. They feel, rather than think, that something is right or wrong. Ideas and inspiration are plentiful, but they tend to lack shape unless there are practical features in other parts of the birthchart.

The native male is a true romantic and a good lover. The tendency to romance, in the sense of making up stories about his beloved, may prevent him from seeing her in a true light; as a result he often falls in love with love. He will make a caring lover, always putting the loved one first.

Suitable careers are found in all the arts, especially as dancer, poet, writer, or actor; those where intuition is used, such as medium or psychic; those where others are cared for, such as nurse, doctor, or priest; and all professions connected with the sea.

The above description will apply substantially to those who have sun, moon, ascendant, or Neptune in Pisces.

Pisces ♓

Keywords: rhythm, liquids, fluidity, abstractions, escape, mystic, pretense, sleep, unworldly, acting, meditation, and all Neptunian words.

The houses

1 This is, naturally, the house concerned with the personality. The vitality and temperament are also shown. In general, it represents the native as seen by other people.

12 This being the natural house of Pisces and Neptune, it shows a need for privacy. It links with hospitals and institutions and service to others, very often in "closed" conditions.

The houses as they fall on a birthchart

The birthchart is divided into "houses," which are numbered from the ascendant in a counterclockwise direction. In the diagram we have shown Aries, the first sign of the zodiac, as the sign for the first house and so on. This is because the first house is the natural house of Aries, but the ascendant may be any sign of the zodiac. The part of a person's life represented by each house is that which has most in common with its natural sign. If you remember this it will help you to define its function.

Rising planets

It should be noted that any planet in the first house will be considered *strong* by virtue of its position. If, in addition, it is within 8 degrees of the ascendant, it is said to be *rising*, and it will be a dominating influence in assessing the psychology of the native.

2 The natural house of Taurus represents the possessions, security, and finance; also, the feelings (possessiveness), activities connected with accumulating possessions or money, and the productiveness of the native.

3 This house indicates communications, near relatives, and short journeys. It will show the native's speech, and adjustment to the immediate environment.

11 The house that indicates groups of friends, clubs, and societies, and intellectual or humanitarian pursuits (Aquarius). Planets in this sign will show that the native is gregarious.

10 The tenth house deals with matters of the public life and career. Planets in this house indicate an interest in social standing and public position (opposite to fourth house).

9 This indicates further education, study in depth, and philosophical concepts. It also represents long-distance travel, the possibility of living abroad, being a good linguist, and dealing with foreigners.

8 This house indicates money from legacies and financial ability in business. It is the house of Scorpio and the planet Pluto, so it also refers to matters of life and death.

7 The house of both emotional and business relationships. The sign on the cusp of the seventh house often indicates the type of marriage partner who will appeal to the native.

4 The fourth house is the house of the home, the parents, and the private life. Planets in this house will suggest a person who would prefer the privacy of home to public life.

5 Having connotations with the sign of Leo and the sun, this house represents creativity, parenthood, and self-expression. It also represents enjoyment, especially in sports and activities.

6 This is the natural house of Virgo and of the planet Mercury. It represents work, service to the community, discipline, authority over others, and the health of the native.

53

The shaping of the chart

Since the planets can fall anywhere on a birthchart, different groupings of planets will sometimes form patterns. Many astrologers take account of the "shaping" of a chart when assessing the personality of the native.

A birthchart where planes are spread fairly evenly all around the chart, probably with no two planets in the same house, will indicate someone of wide interests. This type of shaping is known as a *splash*. An interpretation of the rest of the chart would be necessary before the astrologer would be able to decide whether this person was a talented dabbler or someone who would use all the interests

well, combining them to achieve something worthwhile.

A variety of patterns

In contrast, persons whose planets are all in one area of the chart will have all their interests focused in one direction. This pattern is known as the *bundle*.

A third pattern, the *see-saw*, shows planets in two definite groups opposite each other. In this case, two aspects of the person's life will be equally important and the native may be

▲ *Albert Schweitzer was born in Alsace on January 14, 1875. A brilliant man in many ways, he is perhaps best known for his work at his hospital in Lambarene, where he became a father/priest figure both to his patients and to his helpers.*

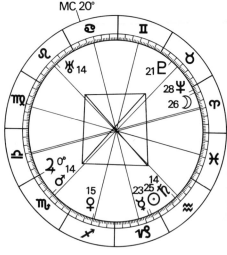

▲ *Schweitzer's chart shows the pattern known as a grand cross, which commonly occurs in the charts of explorers and missionaries. The planet Jupiter in the first house indicates his kindness and sympathy and his breadth of vision.*

able to manipulate both with skill. On the other hand, the person may be unable to reconcile the two aspects.

Some of the other patterns are more difficult to distinguish, and the interpretations given to them often seem a little contrived. However, it does seem to be true that, where all the planets are contained in one half of the chart, one single planet will be very important. It should therefore be given more weight than the others in interpretation.

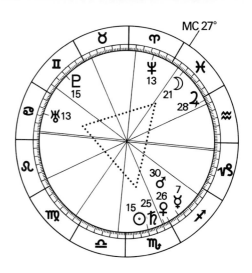

Geometric shapes

Within the overall pattern of a chart, it is sometimes possible to see geometric figures. The charts of Marie Curie and Albert Schweitzer are good examples of this.

Schweitzer's chart has two sets of planets opposing each other. Each forms a square with the other set. This pattern is known as a *grand cross*. It indicates difficulties and often shows up in the charts of people who have deliberately chosen a difficult, albeit rewarding, life.

The chart of Marie Curie shows a *grand trine*. This indicates ease of working in the area represented by the planets involved, which in this case are Uranus, the sun, and the moon.

A further indication of the personality of the native is shown by the position of the majority of the planets in sectors of the chart. If they lie mainly in the south, they will indicate a public personality to whom career and status are important. Northern planets indicate the reverse.

Planets mainly in the east of the chart indicate persons who have their lives in their own hands, while those with planets mainly in the west will be more concerned with the lives of others. The meanings of the houses in these sectors will explain the reason for this.

Marie Curie was born in Warsaw on November 7, 1867. She was inspired to search for the unknown element in material that had been discarded as worthless from a scientific experiment, and discovered radium. In her chart, Uranus (the planet influencing the unusual) is linked with the sun and the moon to form a grand trine. All three planets are in water signs, which are the signs representing inspiration.

How to set up a birth-chart

It is quite an easy matter to erect your own chart by following the steps shown in this section. Should you wish to understand the reasons for each step, you will find them explained in the Reference Section under "Astronomy." The Reference Section also explains where you may obtain the basic information you will need. You will also find valuable helps there. One of these is a table that shows the relation of the local time in various parts of the world to Greenwich Mean Time. Unless you were born in the United Kingdom, it will be necessary for you to find out the relationship between your birth time and Greenwich Mean Time.

Equipment

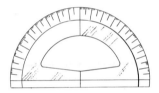

▲ Materials you will need include paper, pencils, a compass, a protractor, and a ruler. You will also need an ephemeris for the year of your birth and a table of houses (see reference section).

The problem of the unknown birth time

Many people do not know their time of birth and think that they cannot have a birthchart done at all, but it is always possible to set up a chart for the day of birth. This will show the signs of the zodiac in which the sun and planets were on that day. It will give only a rough idea of the moon's position. It will not give an ascendant or a mid-heaven (MC), nor will it show which houses the planets were in.

Within these limits such a chart can be useful. But it obviously is not a true representation, which is individual to someone born at a particular time and place. In order to construct such a chart, it is convenient to use a birth time of noon, Greenwich Mean Time.

If you have an idea of the time within an hour or two, it will be worthwhile to choose an approximate time and set up an accurate chart for that time.

Setting up the chart

In order to set up your own chart, you will need the following:

1. An ephemeris for the year of your birth. Most astrologers use *Raphael's Ephemeris* for a given year. It includes all the information necessary for this purpose.

2. A table of houses for northern latitudes, which, by means of a small adjustment can be made to apply to southern latitudes as well.

3. You will need to know the latitude and longitude of your place of birth, which you will be able to find in an atlas or gazetteer.

4. Finally, as already explained, you will need to know the relationship of your local time of birth to Greenwich Mean Time (GMT). Check to see if your birthplace had any time changes at your time of birth.

Drawing up a chart

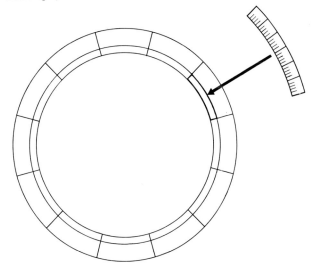

Drawing a chart

You can draw your own birth-chart by the following method. Take a sheet of paper and draw a cirle of 155 mm (6 in.) in diameter. Inside this, draw another circle 130 mm (5 in.) in diameter. Using a protractor, divide the circumference of the circle into twelve equal segments of 30° each. Mark off each of these segments into five degree divisions.

How to begin

Throughout this section, we will take as an example the chart of a child born in New York City at 6:00 A.M. on Christmas Day 1976. By following the various stages, you will be able to substitute your own birth data to find the ascendant and the positions of the lights (sun and moon) and planets.

First, convert your own birth time into Greenwich Mean Time as follows:

1. Write down the latitude and longitude of your place of birth. Do not forget to note whether they are north or south for latitude and east or west for longitude.

2. Now write down your birth time as you know it in hours, minutes, and seconds. Indicate whether it is a.m. or p.m.

3. If your longitude is east *subtract* the number of hours and minutes by which your local time is *faster* than GMT. If your longitude is west, *add* the number of hours and minutes by which your local time is *slower* than GMT.

4. If you were born at a period when daylight saving time was in force, subtract one hour.

5. The result is Greenwich Mean Time and, if it adds up to more

than 24 hours, you should change the date of birth to the next day. (For example, if the child's birth time had added up to 25 hours, it would become 1 A.M. on December 26, 1976). This can be summarized in the case of the chart for the child as in the grid below.

Birth date	*12-25-76*
Birthplace	*New York*
Latitude	*40 43 N*
Longitude	*74 — W*
TIME	*H M S*
Birth time as given	*6 A.M.*
Zone standard (E-W+)	*5*
Summer	
G.M.T.	*11*
G.M.T. date	*12-25-76*

Finding the sidereal time (star time)

Reproduced on this page are two pages from *Raphael's Ephemeris* 1976, open at December. For the purposes of setting up the birthchart, we are only concerned with the line for December 25, which is extended. All we need at this stage is a note of the sidereal time, which is given in the first column as 18 hours 16 minutes 30 seconds.

Make a note of this time as shown on the child's grid, opposite. Add or subtract the difference between noon and the actual GMT time that we have now obtained. In the child's case this is 11:00 A.M., so it is necessary to subtract one hour from the sidereal time at noon. The result is 17 hours 16 minutes 30 seconds. If the time had been 11:00 P.M. GMT, it would have been necessary to add eleven hours to the sidereal time at noon.

The next step is to make an adjustment of ten seconds for each hour's difference from noon. This is known as the *acceleration on the interval*, and a full explanation will be found in the Astronomy section. In this case, we only have to allow for one hour so the difference is ten seconds. Again, this is subtracted because the birth is a.m. For a p.m. birth, the difference is added.

The result of this, 17 hours 16 minutes 20 seconds, is the sidereal time at Greenwich at birth.

The next stage is to make a further adjustment of four minutes for each degree of longitude east or west of Greenwich. In this case, the baby was born in New York at a longitude of 74 degrees west; multiplying by four minutes, we get a total of 296 minutes or 4 hours 56 minutes. Because this is west, it is subtracted from the sidereal time at Greenwich, giving a local sidereal time at birth of 12 hours 20 minutes 20 seconds (written 12H 20M 20S).

If the local sidereal time at birth comes to more than 24 hours, exactly 24 hours should be subtracted from the total. The small grid on the right shows the calculations in detail.

Finding the ascendant

It is now necessary to turn to the table of houses for the latitude in which the native was born.

We have reproduced here a table of houses for New York; you will see that the sidereal time is given in the first column. The columns that follow are headed 10, 11, 12, Ascen., 2, 3. For our purposes, the only column we need is that headed *Ascen.*, which stands for *ascendant*.

D M	D W	Sidereal Time H. M. S.	⊙ Long.	⊙ Dec.	☽ Long.	☽ Lat.	☽ Dec.	MIDNIGHT ☽ Long.	☽ Dec.
1	W	16 41 53	9♐26 0	21 S 52	12♈25 47	1 N51	6 N37	18♈21 12	8 N26
2	Th	16 45 49	10 26 50	22 1	24 15 23	0 N49	10 10	0♉ 8 50	11 47
3	F	16 49 46	11 27 40	22 9	6♉ 2 40	0 S16	13 17	11 55 30	14 40
4	S	16 53 42	12 28 32	22 18	17 49 32	1 19	15 53	23 44 30	16 56
5	⊛	16 57 39	13 29 25	22 25	29 40 45	2 19	17 49	5♊38 30	18 30
6	M	17 1 35	14 30 18	22 32	11♊38 2	3 14	18 59	17 39 31	19 15
7	Tu	17 5 32	15 31 13	22 39	23 43 7	4 0	19 18	29 48 59	19 7
8	W	17 9 29	16 32 9	22 46	5♋57 15	4 36	18 43	12♋ 8 3	18 5
9	Th	17 13 25	17 33 5	22 51	18 21 28	4 59	17 15	24 37 39	16 11
10	F	17 17 22	18 34 3	22 57	0♌56 42	5 8	14 56	7♌18 47	13 39
11	S	17 21 18	19 35 2	23 2	13 44 3	5 2	11 52	20 12 40	10 6
12	⊛	17 25 15	20 36 2	23 6	26 44 52	4 41	8 12	3♍20 49	6 10
13	M	17 29 11	21 37 2	23 11	10♍0 46	4 4	4 N 1	16 44 56	1 N51
14	Tu	17 33 8	22 38 4	23 14	23 33 30	3 13	0 S 24	0♎26 39	2 S 40
15	W	17 37 4	23 39 7	23 17	7♎24 30	2 10	4 56	14 27 6	7 9
16	Th	17 41 1	24 40 11	23 20	21 34 25	0 S 57	9 18	28 46 18	11 20
17	F	17 44 58	25 41 16	23 22	6♏ 2 29	0 N20	13 13	13♏22 30	14 55
18	S	17 48 54	26 42 22	23 24	20 45 48	1 38	16 22	28 11 38	17 34
19	⊛	17 52 51	27 43 28	23 25	5♐17 39	2 49	18 28	13♐ 7 7	19 12
20	M	17 56 47	28 44 36	23 26	20 35 1	3 49	19 18	28 1 13	19 12
21	Tu	18 0 44	29♐45 44	23 26	5♑24 45	4 33	18 47	12♑44 34	18 3
22	W	18 4 40	0♑46 52	23 26	19 59 41	4 58	17 2	27 9 18	15 45
23	Th	18 8 37	1 48 0	23 26	4♒12 45	5 4	14 16	11♒ 9 34	12 36
24	F	18 12 34	2 49 9	23 25	17 59 29	4 52	10 48	24 42 23	8 53
25	S	18 16 30	3 50 18	23 23	1♓18 21	4 24	6 53	7♓47 37	4 51
26	⊛	18 20 27	4 51 27	23 21	14 10 33	3 44	2 S 47	20 27 37	0 S 43
27	M	18 24 23	5 52 36	23 19	26 39 32	3 2	1 N20	2♈49 57	3 N20
28	Tu	18 28 20	6 53 45	23 16	8♈52 30	1 57	5 17	14 49 12	7 10
29	W	18 32 16	7 54 54	23 12	20 46 15	0 N55	8 58	26 41 22	10 40
30	Th	18 36 13	8 55 2	23 8	2♉28 5	0 S 7	12 15	8♉28 29	13 43
31	F	18 40 9	9♑57 11	23 S 4	14♉31 21	1 S 10	15 N 5	20♉15 38	16 N13

FIRST QUARTER—December 28, 7h. 48m. a.m.

D M	♆ Long.	♅ Long.	♄ Long.	♃ Long.	♂ Long.	♀ Long.	☿ Long.	Lunar Aspects. ☉	♇	♆	♅	♄	♃	♂	♀	☿
	° ′	° ′	° ′	° ′	° ′	° ′	° ′									
1	13 ♐ 32	9 ♏ 24	16 ♌ 52	24 ♉ 22	7 ♐ 33	20 ♑ 28	22 ♐ 39	△	☍	△		△	∠	△		
2	13 34	9 28	16 ℞ 51	24 ℞ 15	8 16	21 39	24 10	⚼		⚼			⊻	⚼	□	△
3	13 36	9 31	16 51	24 7	9 0	22 51	25 40				☍					⚼
4	13 39	9 34	16 50	24 0	9 43	24 2	27 10					□				
S	13 41	9 38	16 49	23 53	10 27	25 13	28 ♐ 40		⚼				●		△	
6	13 43	9 41	16 48	23 45	11 10	26 25	0 ♑ 10	☍	△	☍		⚹		☍	⚼	
7	13 45	9 44	16 47	23 38	11 54	27 36	1 39				⚼		⊻			
8	13 48	9 47	16 46	23 31	12 38	28 47	3 7				△	∠	∠			☍
9	13 50	9 50	16 45	23 25	13 22	29 ♑ 57	4 34		□			⊻	⚹			
10	13 52	9 54	16 44	23 18	14 5	1 ♒ 8	6 1	⚼		⚼				⚼	☍	
11	13 54	9 57	16 42	23 11	14 49	2 19	7 27	△	⚹	△	□	☌		△		
S	13 57	10 0	16 41	23 5	15 33	3 29	8 51		∠				□			⚼
13	13 59	10 3	16 39	22 59	16 17	4 40	10 14		⊻	□	⚹	⊻		□		△
14	14 1	10 6	16 37	22 52	17 1	5 50	11 36	□			∠		△		⚼	
15	14 3	10 9	16 35	22 46	17 45	7 1	12 55		☌	⚹	⊻	∠	⚼		△	□
16	14 6	10 12	16 33	22 41	18 29	8 11	14 13	⚹				⚹		⚹		
17	14 8	10 15	16 31	22 35	19 13	9 21	15 27	∠		∠	●			∠	□	
18	14 10	10 18	16 29	22 29	19 58	10 31	16 39	⊻	⊻	⊻		□	☍	⊻		⚹
S	14 12	10 21	16 27	22 24	20 42	11 41	17 47		∠		⊻				⚹	∠
20	14 15	10 23	16 24	22 19	21 26	12 50	18 51		⚹	☌	∠	△		☌		⊻
21	14 17	10 26	16 22	22 14	22 10	14 0	19 49	☌			⚹	⚼	⚼		∠	
22	14 19	10 30	16 19	22 9	22 55	15 9	20 43		□	⊻			△	⊻	⊻	☌
23	14 21	10 32	16 16	22 4	23 39	16 19	21 30	⊻		∠	□			∠		
24	14 23	10 34	16 14	22 0	24 24	17 28	22 10	∠	△	⚹		☍	□		☌	⊻
25	14 25	10 37	16 11	21 55	25 8	18 37	22 41	⚹	⚼					⚹		
S	14 28	10 40	16 8	21 51	25 53	19 46	23 4			□	△				⊻	∠
27	14 30	10 42	16 5	21 47	26 37	20 54	23 17				⚼	⚼	⚹	□		⚹
28	14 32	10 45	16 2	21 44	27 22	22 3	23 19	□	☍	△			∠		∠	
29	14 34	10 47	15 58	21 40	28 7	23 11	23 ℞ 9					△	⊻		⚹	□
30	14 36	10 50	15 55	21 37	28 52	24 19	22 49			⚼				△		
31	14 ♐ 38	10 ♏ 52	15 ♌ 52	21 ♉ 33	29 ♐ 36	25 ♒ 27	22 ♑ 16	△			☍	□		⚼		

Last Quarter—December 14, 10*h*. 14*m*. *a.m.*

◀ *Two pages showing the sidereal time and position of the planets on Christmas Day, 1976. Reproduced from the 1976* Raphael's Ephemeris, *© W. Foulsham & Co. Ltd.*

	H	M	S
Sid time noon G.M.T.	18	16	30
Interval a.m.			
TO/FROM noon p.m.	1	—	—
Result	17	16	30
Acceleration			10
Sid. time at Greenwich at birth	17	16	20
Longitude equivalent (E + W −)	4	56	
LOCAL SID. TIME AT BIRTH	12	20	20
Subtract 24 hrs. if necessary			

▼ *John Harrison's marine chronometer, the first successful navigational aid to determine longitude. There was nothing accurate enough for this purpose until the 18th century.*

Still working with the child's chart, we locate the sidereal time at which we arrived — 12 hours 20 minutes 20 seconds — and we find that the nearest time given is 12 hours 22 minutes 2 seconds. This gives an ascendant of 15 degrees 38 minutes and, at the top of the column under the heading *Ascen.* we see the sign for Sagittarius.

Although we are concerned only with the ascendant at the moment, to save turning to the table of houses again, we should note the column headed 10, which will be the midheaven. (MC). With a sidereal time of 12 hours 22 minutes 2 seconds, the figure shown under column 10 is 6 degrees and the sign shown under 10 is the sign for Libra. Before going back to the ephemeris, we will note that the MC will be 6 degrees Libra.

Example

Let us suppose that the chart we have already set up is for a child born at 6 a.m. on December 25, 1976, still at longitude 74° west, but at latitude 40° south. The workings are exactly the same as before, so the local sidereal time is 12 hours 20 minutes 20 seconds less 12 hours; i.e. 0 hours 20 minutes 20 seconds.

The New York table of houses shows the nearest time is 0 hours 22 minutes 2 seconds. Following this across, the ascendant column shows 23 degrees 24 minutes Cancer. For the southern latitude, this will be 23 degrees 24 minutes Capricorn. Under the column heading 10, we see 6 degrees Aries, so the midheaven for the southern birth will be 6 degrees Libra.

Marking in the ascendant

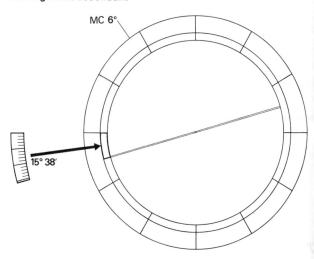

MC 6°

15° 38'

How to find the ascendant for a birth in the southern hemisphere

We have been using the tables for northern latitudes, but, by a very simple adjustment, this book will also serve for southern latitudes. The adjustment is as follows:

1. Deduct or add (whichever is the most convenient) 12 hours to local sidereal time at birth.

2. Note the degrees of the ascendant for the time obtained, but the sign will be the opposite zodiacal sign of the one shown.

TABLES OF HOUSES FOR NEW YORK, *Latitude* 40° 43' N.																			
Sidereal Time.	10 ♈	11 ♉	12 ♊	Ascen ♋	2 ♌	3 ♍	Sidereal Time.	10 ♉	11 ♊	12 ♋	Ascen ♌	2 ♍	3 ♎	Sidereal Time.	10 ♊	11 ♋	12 ♌	Ascen ♍	2 ♍	3 ♎
H. M. S.	°	°	°	° ° °	°	°	H. M. S.	°	°	°	°	°	°	H. M. S.	°	°	°	° ° '	°	°
0 0 0	0	6	15	18 53	8	1	1 51 37	0	6	11	11	8	2 28	3 51 15	0	5	7	4	32	28 27
0 3 40	1	7	16	19 38	9	2	1 55 27	1	7	12	11	53	3 29	3 55 25	1	6	8	5	22	29 28
0 7 20	2	8	17	20 23	10	3	1 59 17	2	8	13	12	38	4 ♎	3 59 36	2	6	8	6	10	♎ 29
0 11 0	3	9	18	21 9	11	4	2 3 8	3	9	14	13	22	5 1	4 3 48	3	7	9	7	0	1 ♏
0 14 41	4	11	19	21 55	12	5	2 6 59	4	10	15	14	8	5 2	4 8 0	4	8	10	7	49	2 1
0 18 21	5	12	20	22 40	12	5	2 10 51	5	11	15	14	53	6 3	4 12 13	5	9	11	8	40	3 2
0 22 2	6	13	21	23 24	13	6	2 14 44	6	12	16	15	39	7 4	4 16 26	6	10	12	9	30	4 3
0 25 42	7	14	22	24 8	14	7	2 18 37	7	13	17	16	24	8 4	4 20 40	7	11	13	10	19	4 4
0 29 23	8	15	23	24 54	15	8	2 22 31	8	14	18	17	10	9 5	4 24 55	8	12	14	11	10	5 5
0 33 4	9	16	23	25 37	15	9	2 26 25	9	15	19	17	56	10 6	4 29 10	9	13	15	12	0	6 6
0 36 45	10	17	24	26 22	16	10	2 30 20	10	16	20	18	41	10 7	4 33 26	10	14	16	12	51	7 7
0 40 26	11	18	25	27 5	17	11	2 34 16	11	17	20	19	27	11 8	4 37 42	11	15	16	13	41	8 8
0 44 8	12	19	26	27 50	18	12	2 38 13	12	18	21	20	14	12 9	4 41 59	12	16	17	14	32	9 9
0 47 50	13	20	27	28 33	19	13	2 42 10	13	19	22	21	0	13 10	4 46 16	13	17	18	15	23	10 10
0 51 32	14	21	28	29 18	19	13	2 46 8	14	19	23	21	47	14 11	4 50 34	14	18	19	16	14	11 11
0 55 14	15	22	28	0 ♌ 3	20	14	2 50 7	15	20	24	22	33	15 12	4 54 52	15	19	20	17	5	12 12
0 58 57	16	23	29	0 46	21	15	2 54 7	16	21	25	23	20	16 13	4 59 10	16	20	21	17	56	13 13

60

The Magi, from a sixth century mosaic in Ravenna. The Wise Men were astronomers, who observed the heavens, and also astrologers, since they correctly interpreted what they saw.

◀ Tables of houses for New York. Reproduced from the 1976 Raphael's Ephemeris, © W. Foulsham & Co. Ltd.

TABLES OF HOUSES FOR NEW YORK, Latitude 40° 43′ N.

Sidereal Time.	10	11	12	Ascen	2	3	Sidereal Time.	10	11	12	Ascen	2	3	Sidereal Time.	10	11	12	Ascen	2	3
H. M. S.	12	0	0	0 29 21 11	7 15	24	H. M. S.	13 51 37	0 25 15	85 16 27	H. M. S.	15 51 15	0 21 13	9 8 27							

Reproduced from the 1976 Raphael's Ephemeris, © W. Foulsham & Co. Ltd.

Drawing in the houses

Going back to our original chart, you will remember that we had an ascendant of 15 degrees 38 minutes Sagittarius. This is the degree that is rising in the east (on the left-hand side of the chart). Put the sign (or glyph) for Sagittarius in the first house, as shown in the diagram, and continue the signs in their correct order from Sagittarius in counterclockwise round the chart. After Pisces, you start again at Aries and continue in order until Sagittarius is reached.

Each of the houses has been sectioned into five degree intervals, so you will easily see where fifteen degrees comes. Put a mark at the point of 15 degrees 38 minutes (as nearly as you can judge) in each house all around the chart. Then join these marks by ruling straight across the chart so that 15 degrees 38 minutes Sagittarius is joined to 15 degrees 38 minutes Gemini, and so on. The first line, joining the ascendant to the decendant, should be made thicker than the other lines for ease in recognition. Under the sign Sagittarius, insert the number of degrees, i.e. 15° 38'.

Glyphs of the signs

♈	**Aries**	♎	**Libra**
♉	**Taurus**	♏	**Scorpio**
♊	**Gemini**	♐	**Sagittarius**
♋	**Cancer**	♑	**Capricorn**
♌	**Leo**	♒	**Aquarius**
♍	**Virgo**	♓	**Pisces**

Marking in the signs

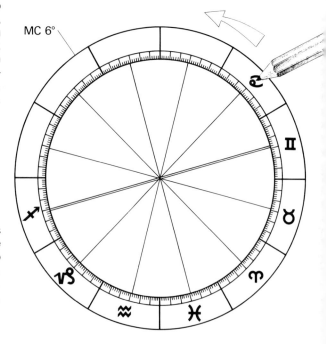

MC 6°

The cusps

The lines defining the houses are known as cusps. The house from the ascendant to the cusp in Capricorn is the first house, and so on, counterclockwise. Finally, mark the MC at 6° Libra, as shown in the diagram.

Putting in the planets

Now turn back to the pages from the ephemeris for 1976 shown on page 59 and follow the extended line for 25th December. We are interested only in the columns headed Long. (Longitude). It is accurate enough to take the nearest degree. Remember, there are 60 minutes in one degree.

You will see that under the column headed Long. at December 25th, it says 3 degrees 50 minutes 18 seconds. Running your eye up that column, you will see that the sun moved into the sign of Capricorn three days before, so on the 25th the sun is at 3° 50' 18" of Capricorn at noon. As the child was born only one hour before noon, the nearest degree will be 4°. Insert the symbol for the sun at that position on the chart with the figure 4 beside it.

The position for the moon is given in the column headed Long., which shows that at noon the moon was at 1° 18' 21" of Pisces. However, the moon changes position much faster than the sun, so here we need to be more accurate. The moon's position at noon on the previous day was 17° 59' 29" Aquarius, so it has moved from about 18° Aquarius to about 1° Pisces in 24 hours. This is equal to 13° (remember there are 30° to each sign) or about half a degree an hour. The child was born one hour before noon, GMT, so we can deduct half a degree from noon on the 25th. This still gives us 1° Pisces to the nearest degree. The symbol for the moon is inserted opposite 1° of Pisces with the figure 1 beside it, as shown in the diagram.

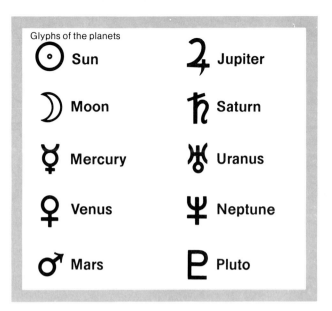

Glyphs of the planets

☉ Sun   ♃ Jupiter

☽ Moon   ♄ Saturn

☿ Mercury   ♅ Uranus

♀ Venus   ♆ Neptune

♂ Mars   ♇ Pluto

Marking in the planets

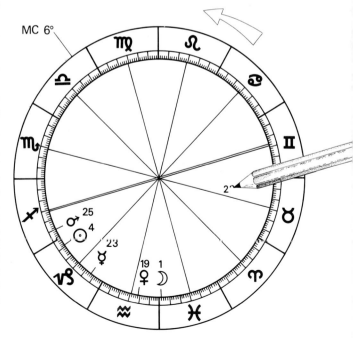

The positions of the other planets are on the right-hand page. They start on the far right with the planet Mercury, working in towards the center. Remembering that the child was born one hour before noon, the nearest degree is 23 degrees Capricorn (you will see the Capricorn sign opposite December 6, the day on which Mercury first moved into Capricorn). Follow the December 25 line across the right-hand page to get the positions of all the planets, up to and including Neptune, and insert them on the chart.

Checking

We have now completed the setting up of the whole birthchart and can begin to prepare for interpretation. Before doing so, make sure that the birthchart is set up correctly by checking three things:

1. The sun will be near the ascendant for a birth at about 6 a.m. It will be near the midheaven for a birth about 12 noon, near the descendant for a birth about 6 p.m. and near the undersky (IC-Imum Coeli) for a birth about 12 midnight. This is a quick check that will enable you to ascertain that the ascendant is correct.

2. The planet Mercury should never be more than 28° away from the sun.

3. The planet Venus should never be more than 48° away from the sun. This does not mean that Venus cannot be nearer the sun than Mercury.

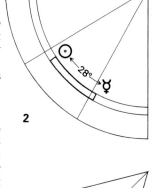

2

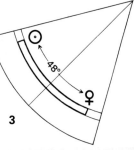

3

Pluto

Because Pluto is so slow-moving, its positions for the whole year are given separately, as shown. You will see the nearest day to December 25 is December 26 when Pluto's longitude was 14° 4′ Libra, so 14° Libra will be the nearest degree. Insert Pluto's position at 14° Libra.

THE POSITION OF PLUTO (♇) IN 1976.

Date	Long.	Lat.	Dec.	Date	Long.	Lat.	Dec.	Date	Long.	Lat.	Dec.
	o '	o '	o '		o '	o '	o '		o '	o '	o '
Jan. 1	11≏40	16 N53	10 N55	May 10	9 Ω20	17 N22	12 N15	Sept. 17	10≏56	16 N27	10 N48
11	11 42	16 58	11 0	20	9 R 9	17 18	12 15	27	11 19	16 26	10 39
21	11 R42	17 4	11 5	30	9 2	17 13	12 14	Oct. 7	11 42	16 26	10 30
31	11 38	17 10	11 12	June 9	8 57	17 8	12 12	17	12 5	16 27	10 22
Feb. 10	11 30	17 15	11 19	19	8 D56	17 3	12 7	27	12 28	16 29	10 15
20	11 20	17 19	11 27	29	8 57	16 58	12 2	Nov. 6	12 50	16 32	10 9
Mar. 1	11 7	17 23	11 35	July 9	9 3	16 53	11 55	16	13 10	16 35	10 5
11	10 52	17 26	11 44	19	9 11	16 48	11 47	26	13 27	16 39	10 2
21	10 36	17 28	11 51	29	9 23	16 43	11 38	Dec. 6	13 42	16 44	10 1
31	10 20	17 28	11 58	Aug. 8	9 37	16 38	11 29	16	13 55	16 49	10 1
Apr. 10	10 3	17 28	12 5	18	9 54	16 34	11 19	26	14 4	16 54	10 3
20	9 47	17 27	12 9	28	10 13	16 31	11 9	31	14≏ 7	16 N58	10 N 4
30	9≏32	17 N25	12 N13	Sept. 7	10≏34	16 N29	10 N58				

▲ *The position of Pluto in 1976. Reproduced from the 1976 Raphael's Ephemeris. © W. Foulsham & Co. Ltd. In some years, the position of Pluto is printed at the bottom of the page for each month.*

▶ *The planetary system as Ptolemy conceived it in the second century A.D. It shows the unmoving Earth at the center surrounded by the spheres of the moon, the sun, and the five known planets.*

Preparing for interpretation

Astrologers take many points into account in interpreting a birthchart. All of them will consider the basic factors, but beyond these there are new theories being introduced and tested all the time. Astrologers tend to adopt the ones that appeal to them. There is nothing static about modern astrology; it may owe a debt to the past, but there is no doubt it is a living science. In this book we can only consider the basic approach to interpretation, but you will find further reading suggested in the Reference section.

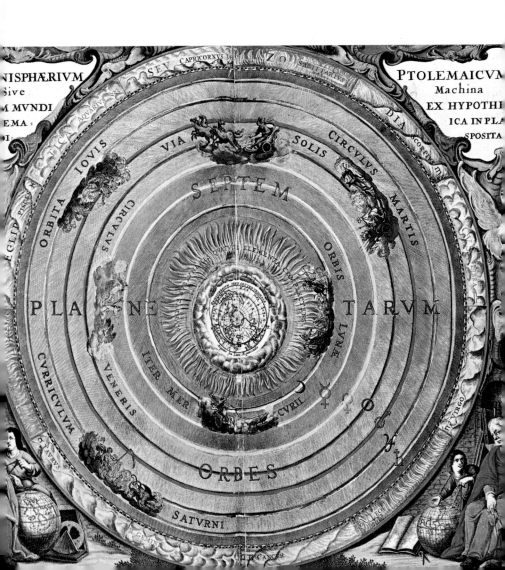

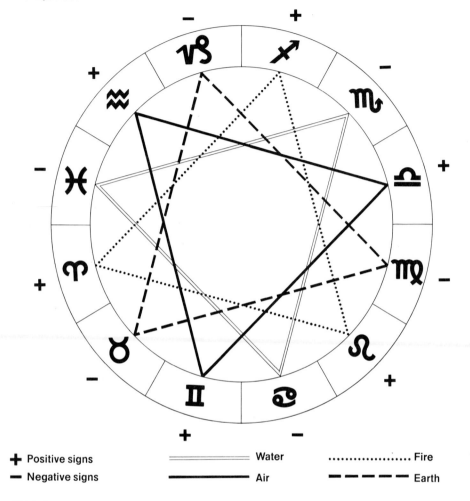

+ Positive signs ===== Water .... Fire
— Negative signs ——— Air — — — — Earth

The psychological mixture

Before we begin the interpretation itself, we should make notes of various factors in the chart. These are as follows:

1. positive and negative signs

2. fire, earth, air, and water signs

3. cardinal, fixed, and mutable signs.

The charts on this page will show you which categories the signs fall into, but a fuller explanation will be found on page 25. See if you can work them out for yourself before reading on.

We will continue to use as an example the chart of the child born on December 25, 1976. In the child's chart, the sun is in a negative, earth, cardinal sign (Capricorn). The moon is in a negative, water, mutable sign (Pisces). Mercury is in a negative, earth, cardinal sign (Capricorn). Venus is in a positive, air, fixed sign (Aquarius). Mars is in a

| Cardinal | Fixed | Mutable |

---

positive, fire, mutable sign (Sagittarius). Jupiter is in a negative, earth, fixed sign (Taurus). Saturn is in a positive, fire, fixed sign (Leo). Uranus is in a negative, water, fixed sign (Scorpio). Neptune is in a positive, fire, mutable sign (Sagittarius). Pluto is in a positive, air, cardinal sign (Libra).

Positive and negative

This means that there are five planets in positive signs and five in negative signs, so there is a good balance between extroversion and introversion. Both the ascendant and the MC are in positive signs, so there should be a slight tendency towards the extrovert.

Triplicities

With regard to the triplicities, there are three planets in fire signs, three in earth signs, two in air signs, and two in water signs. Again, we have a very good balance, with the ascendant in a fire sign indicating that the tendency will be towards energy and enthusiasm.

Quadruplicities

The pattern of a good balance is repeated yet again when we see that there are three planets in cardinal signs, four in fixed signs and three in mutable signs. Here, the balance is slightly towards fixity, so we can say that, despite the outgoing and active nature, there is a tendency to be cautious.

Strong in its own sign

The next thing we should consider and make a note of is whether any of the planets are strong in their own signs. In this particular chart, there is no planet in its own sign, but it is worth noting that the sun is in Capricorn (ruled by Saturn) and Saturn is in Leo (ruled by the sun). This is said to bring the two planets into mutual reception. We will look at this point again when we come to consider the aspects.

Ruling planets

The planet that rules the ascending sign is said to be the ruling planet, and this should also be noted. In this case, the ascendant is in Sagittarius, which is ruled by Jupiter; this makes Jupiter an important planet in the chart. We will consider this in more detail in the discussion that follows. Each of the planets will be considered separately.

The birthchart of Neil Armstrong

▶ Neil Armstrong's chart is a good example of a chart with planets strong in the signs that they are said to rule. Here, the sun is in its natural house of Leo, Mercury is in Virgo and Saturn is in Capricorn.
    From this, one would interpret that the personality (sun), mentality (Mercury) and sense of responsibility and reliability (Saturn) are all important elements of his character.

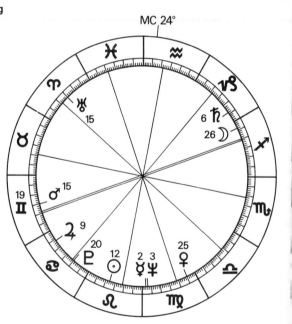

Interpreting the chart

There are various ways of tackling the interpretation. Some people like to analyze under different headings, considering the factors that will show specific areas, such as health, type of mentality, or career choices. Most of these can be indicated by more than one factor, so we will consider the ascendant, sun, and moon in connection with each and then the planets, with particular reference to their own fields of influence.

The ascendant and the sun are both important factors in interpretation. The ascendant shows the apparent personality and the sun shows the basic personality. The moon will also be a strong factor, as it shows the emotional content and the subconscious feelings.

ASC

With the example chart, we have a Sagittarian ascendant. Read again the description of Sagittarius and make brief notes of the salient points. These might read as follows:
Personality: outgoing, optimistic, freedom-loving; sees the overall picture and not the details. Health: likely to be good, but needs exercise and fresh air. Bilious if over-indulgent. Careers: sports, acting, philosophy, law.

Now, consider the sun in Capricorn in the first house. Read again the descriptions of Capricorn and the first house. Your notes might read as follows:
Basic personality: ambitious, practical, patient. Self-oriented (first house). Mentality: slow to learn but thorough. Will get to the top by plodding. Health: sturdy, but must be made to relax and not bottle up emotions. Beware of chills. Careers: good in any executive or administrative job. Gets on well with older people.

The moon is in Pisces in the third house. Your notes for this might be as follows:
Personality: adaptability adaptable, emotionally receptive, and intuitive. Very firmly attached to family and near relations. Mentality: tends to daydream but could be a fictional writer or poet (third house indicates communications, as well as near neighbors).

The completed birthchart

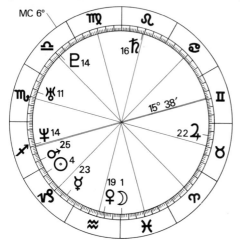

MC 6°

♀ in ♒ in 3

ate in the sign and house in which it is located in the chart. Your notes might read as follows:

Personal relationships: important, especially for family and close friends (third house), but personal freedom is extremely important. Will have lots of acquaintances, but may appear cool and find difficulty in being close to people.

Again, we see the pattern of balance with an ascendant in fire, sun in earth, and moon in water signs. So far, we have a mentality that is wide-ranging, day-dreamy (or intuitive), and slow to learn but thorough. Which is the strongest of these characteristics? We shall see when we come to consider the planet of the mentality, Mercury.

will be a tendency to bottle up emotions.

Carry on making notes in the same way on all the planets in order, considering with each how its special function will oper-

♂ in ♐ in 1

Vitality: very good (in fire sign and in first house). Energy: will be directed toward achieving his own ends in various and wide-ranging ways.

☿ in ♑ in 2

Make notes on Mercury, remembering that this is the planet of communications of all kinds. Mercury is in Capricorn in the second house, so the notes could read:
The mind will not be quick but will learn thoroughly. In the house of possessions, it will be oriented towards making money and achieving a good position (reinforcing the Capricorn ambition). The nervous system will be strong but there

70

♇ in ♎ in 10

At this stage, there is nothing to indicate that Pluto is other than a generation influence, but any planet in the tenth house is likely to relate to career. There could be many changes in this field.

♃ in ♉ in 6

Relaxation is found in work (sixth house) relating to artistic or other Taurean pursuits.

♄ in ♌ in 9

Capacity for leadership shown in very responsible and hardworking ways; a practical organizer. Capable of carrying out big projects; travel and dealing with foreigners indicated.

The three outer planets, Uranus, Neptune, and Pluto, are slow-moving and will be in the same sign for a long time, indicating a generation rather than a personal influence.

♅ in ♏ in 11

Uranus is in its natural house, the eleventh, so it is more than just a generation influence. This emphasizes the need for freedom, which will be passionately sought. Will be gregarious and humanitarian, as long as freedom is not threatened.

♆ in ♐ in 12

Neptune is also in its natural house, the twelfth, so intuition possibly mediumistic ability) is present. In the sign of Sagittarius (emphasis on hips and thighs) there is likely to be a love of dancing. People who are strongly Neptunian usually have a marvelous sense of rhythm. Planet in twelfth indicates a necessity for privacy at times. This may tie in with the feeling that freedom is important.

MC in ♎ in 10

Career: likely to be in the area of relationships as a middleman, such as a courier, interpreter, broker, or artists' representative.

At this stage, we could expand the notes by further reference to the nature of the planets, signs, and houses. A recognizable human being would then begin to emerge. However, there is one further stage we should consider before attempting a full interpretation. This is an examination of how the planets interact with one another.

The aspects

The way planets interact can be seen from the type of aspect they make. Planets are said to be in aspect if they are within a significant distance of each other. Some astrologers use many different aspects, but we shall cover only those that are considered to be the strongest.

1. The Conjunction This occurs when two planets are very close together. Most astrologers allow a conjunction within eight degrees (this is known as an orb of eight degrees). More often than not, the planets are both in the same sign and house, so it is understandable that they would have a lot of characteristics in common. Two planets in conjunction usually work well together, depending on the sign and house they are in. For instance, Jupiter conjunct Saturn in Virgo in the tenth house would indicate that work is enjoyed and, at the same time that there is a sense of responsibility and there is capability.

2. The Opposition This, as its name implies, occurs when two planets are opposite each other (180° apart). Again, an orb of eight degrees is allowed. This was once considered a difficult aspect; but if it is used well, it can make for a good balance. Again, the signs and houses involved are important. In the

opposition it is usual for both signs to be either positive or both negative, so that they have much in common.

3. The Trine The planets are 120° (or four signs) apart from each other — an orb of six degrees is allowed, so that if they were 114° to 126° apart they would still be considered to be in trine. They work easily together because they are in signs of the same triplicity.

4. The Square The planets are 90° apart — an orb of six degrees being allowed. These planets will work together with difficulty as they will be of the same quadruplicity.

This means that they will not be in signs that have an element in common.

5. The Sextile The planets are 60° apart, an orb of four degrees being allowed. Although a weaker aspect than the trine, planets in

sextile work well together. As with the opposition, the two planets will both be in positive signs or both in negative signs.

Disassociated aspects

It is possible for aspects to occur when a planet is at the very end of its sign and the planet that it is aspecting is at the very beginning of its sign. For example, Mars at 27° Sagittarius would make a trine aspect to Saturn at two degrees Taurus, but they would not then be in the same triplicity, Mars would be in a fire sign and Saturn in an earth sign. When this occurs, it is known as a disassociated aspect and it will have a weaker effect, either for ease or difficulty of working.

Astrologers do not refer to aspects as good and bad; modern psychology has enabled us to understand that we develop our characters through the ways we encounter difficulties, and any aspect that helps us to develop our character is not wholly bad. Similarly, an "easy" chart can produce a "the world owes me a living" attitude. Such persons expect everything to come easily and are likely to complain bitterly if it does not; good aspects are certainly not good for them. Most birthcharts show a mixture of both easy and difficult aspects, the best combination.

Working out the aspects

We will now work out the aspects as shown in the child's chart. The easiest way to do this is to remember that the maximum orb allowed is eight degrees. If the difference of degree between two planets is more than eight degrees, we can assume that there is no aspect between them.

Follow the grid below to remind yourself of the order in which to work. The first sign in the vertical column is for the sun, so we will look at aspects to sun first. The signs across the

chart start with the sun and then the moon.

The sun is at four degrees and the moon at one degree, so there is an orb of only three degrees and it is likely that they are in aspect. Count the number of degrees between them (remembering that each house or sign is exactly 30°) and you will see that they are 58° apart, so they are in sextile to each other. We note the sign for Sextile on the grid in the square under moon sign and look at the sun's

aspect to Mercury. With sun at four degrees and Mercury at 23°, there is an orb of 19°; so there is no aspect between them. Venus is at 19° and sun at four degrees, so the orb is 15° and there is no aspect. The sun and Mars are only nine degrees apart, but this is just too big an orb for the conjunction; so there is no aspect. This would have been an example of a disassociated aspect if the orb had been less. (Astrologers use the expressions "within orb" and "out of orb").

Continue in this way looking at the other planets in order in comparison to the sun. You should find that none of them make aspects. However, you may remember that we noted that Saturn was in mutual reception to the sun. This is considered to have the same effect as a conjunction, so we will note MR on the grid.

Now we go to the next line on the grid and consider the aspects to the moon. You should find that all of them are out of orb, and there are no aspects. Mars appears to be in orb, as there are only six degrees between 25° of one sign and one degree of another; but this is a sextile aspect, and the orb for the sextile is only four degrees.

Continue in the same way across each line of the grid, not forgetting the aspects to the ascendant and MC. Your grid should now look like the one on this page. Now let us interpret these results.

An aspect grid

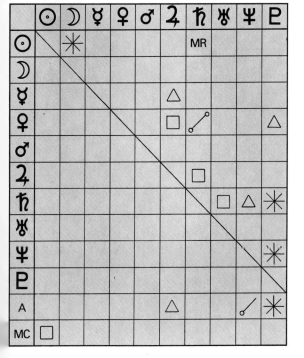

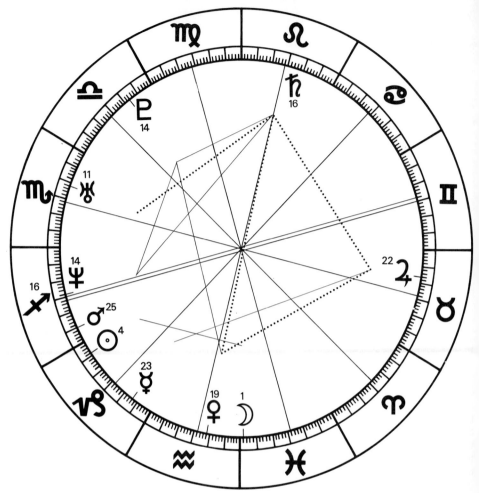

The completed birthchart showing the aspects

Drawing the aspect lines on the chart

To complete the child's birthchart, draw in the aspect lines.

If you use pens of two different colors, you can see at a glance which are easy and which are difficult aspects.

First mark a clear dot on the inside of the glyph of each planet. Take the colored pen you have decided to use for the easy aspects and draw straight lines between the dots, marking the positions of each pair of planets that are in trine or sextile to each other, as marked on the aspect grid. Thus, there will be lines from sun to moon, Mercury to Jupiter, Venus to Pluto, Saturn to Neptune, Saturn to Pluto and Neptune to Pluto. Using the other color, draw lines between each pair of planets that are in square to each other; that is, Venus to Jupiter, Venus to Saturn, Jupiter to Saturn, and Saturn to Uranus.

How to interpret the aspects

When interpreting the aspects, it is important to remember that the planets will work in the ways that are appropriate to them. The sun, moon, and ascendant express the fundamental parts of the personality, so more weight should be given to aspects to them than to the other planets. The sun and moon are in sextile, which is an easy aspect. It is important that the basic personality (sun) and the subconscious or instinctive nature (moon) should be compatible. When they are not, there will be a dichotomy that the native may find difficult to reconcile.

An integrated personality. Sense of responsibility and hardheadedness, softened by an awareness that intuition can be as valid as practicality.

This will strengthen the Capricornian qualities of the sun sign practicality and responsibility and also strengthen Saturn's characteristics (patience, ambition). Native likely to achieve success by sheer hard work.

☿ △ ♃

Enjoys mental pursuits. Mind wide-ranging. Lively sense of fun.

♀ □ ♃

Love life likely to be of an "easy come, easy go" variety. Affairs not taken seriously.

♀ ☌ ♄

Tendency to sacrifice love life to ambitions. This also indicates possible selfishness in close relationships.

♀ △ ♇

Financial ability, especially with Pluto in the Venusian sign of Libra.

♃ □ ♄

Restless; does not recognize limitations and must be doing something practical. Relaxes in working ways.

♄ □ ♅

Tension common, possibly between sense of duty and own freedom.

♄ △ ♆

Intuition and imagination controlled and put to work (emphasizes sun/moon).

♄ ✳ ♇

Generation influence, but shows that he can break away from frustrations and limitations.

♆ ✳ ♇

Uses intuition well.

ASC △ ♄

Lots of common sense and practical ability in a very personal way. Strongly ambitious.

ASC ☌ ♆

Necessity for privacy for development of intuition.

ASC ✳ ♇

Accepts changes well.

MC □ ☉

Difficulty in obtaining objectives.

Types of interpretation

We now have enough details to begin a simple interpretation of the child's basic character and personality. Do not forget that this is a birthchart (i.e. the personality at the moment of birth); but nothing stands still, and the child will continue to grow and develop. A description given to the parents at this point would be somewhat different from one supplied to the adult native. Though the basic characteristics remain the same, the personality traits will be modified by experience and training.

An interpretation done for anyone other than the native (e.g. a prospective employer) would again be different. It would highlight the mentality and capacity for hard work, but would not mention things that do not concern the other person. Astrology is so revealing that some people consider it unethical to divulge the interpretation of a birthchart to anyone other than the native, it should certainly never be done without the permission of the subject.

Interpretation to the child's parents

We will now consider the child's chart as if we were giving advice to the child's parents from it. You will note that our interpretation now emphasizes several things that are obviously very strong in this child's personality. This is a common finding when analyzing a chart. The following is the kind of interpretation a practicing astrologer might send

to the parents of this child.

Your child has a well-balanced personality, neither too brash nor too shy, with an interesting mixture of energy, practicality, and

adaptability. He will have an optimistic and enthusiastic nature and will be interested in a wide range of things. Despite his enthusiasm, he has a practical basic personality that will keep his feet on the ground and will enable him to reach his objectives by sheer hard work, patience, and perseverance.

He may not learn or move quickly, but whatever he does will be done thoroughly. As a child, he may often exasperate you by his slowness when you are in a hurry; but you will find that he does get there in his own maddening, thorough way. As he is also likely to be obstinate, it would be as well to let him take his time rather than wear yourself out trying to change him. Apart from this, you will find him amenable to discipline.

Unconsciously, he is very receptive and intuitive and can be more easily hurt than he will ever show. He needs to be encouraged to express his feelings; otherwise he may tend to

suppress them. This could lead to health difficulties in later life.

His health and vitality are likely to be good, but he really needs exercise and fresh air; you will need to guard him against chills. Walking, running, and swimming are all excellent for him. There is a possibility that he will enjoy rich food and he could easily become bilious if he overindulges.

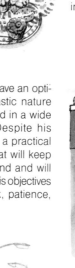

He will not be the sort of person who can relax by being quiet. He is only really relaxed when he is doing something and, therefore, really needs to tire out his body with physical exercise.

With regard to his education, do not be discouraged by his slowness to learn. He will digest what he learns very thoroughly and, although he may be interested in many things on a superficial level, he will be capable of deep study when the subject really catches his imagination. He will be both ambitious and hardworking and will use a good education to the fullest extent. In fact, the chart indicates that he will have a very successful career, possibly in a field where he can use his strong powers of practical organization, a field that requires his type of wide-ranging vision. His career is likely to be financially rewarding and may involve traveling, living abroad, or dealing with foreigners. If he shows an aptitude for languages, this should be encouraged, as his career could easily be that of a diplomat or interpreter. Other careers that are likely to appeal include the law and the church.

His personal relationships with his family and close friends will be very good, but it is quite possible that he will opt for a career rather than for a home life of his own. He has a great feeling for personal freedom and his life will be very firmly in his own hands; no one else will be allowed to control it.

He will have a great many friends and acquaintances, but may find difficulty in expressing affection, due to a fear that his freedom is threatened if he gets too close. You should not worry if he shows that he likes to be entirely by himself at times. Privacy is necessary to him, but there will be plenty of other times when he is gregarious.

As he is such a practical person, it is important that he should develop the intuitive side of his nature. Never discourage him by laughing at his imagination; an awareness that intuition can be as valid as hard facts will be valuable in preventing him from becoming too down-to-earth in

his outlook. His hunches will normally turn out to be correct.

His tensions are likely to be caused by a restless attitude. He finds it difficult to recognize his limitations, realizes that his results are obtained only by sheer plodding, and may sometimes find that his feelings for discipline fight against his equally strong urge for freedom.

He reacts well to change, however, and despite the tension is able to break away from frustrating and limiting circumstances.

Although this is only a short analysis from basic data, it will give the parents the information they require: how to bring up this particular child to develop his whole personality and to appreciate his needs for health and education purposes.

By following a similar pattern, you should now be able to interpret your own birthchart.

Conclusions

In attempting to interpret your own birthchart, or that of someone well-known to you, it is necessary to maintain a detached attitude. Do not let your conclusions be colored by your feelings. Although you will probably get some initial surprises, you may find, on consideration, that these are very revealing, and they may open up new vistas — perhaps encouraging you to take up a hobby

(or even a career) that you would not otherwise have considered.

With the help of astrology, it is possible to explore the psychological makeup of a person in some depth. Those who already work in the field of psychology will find it a useful additional tool.

In this small book it has not been possible to do more than touch on this very wide subject. We have not been able to give instructions on assessing future trends, for instance.

Although this is by no means the most important application of astrology, many people think of forecasting as the primary role of an astrologer. If you want

to try it, there is no shortage of information.

The reference section lists the names of books that will help you.

Joining an astrological society is one sure way of getting help and encouragement. Even if you cannot attend the meetings, you can be put in touch with astrologers in your area and receive literature and replies to your questions.

Astrologers come in all shapes and sizes and at all levels of knowledge. You will find plenty of beginners, like yourself, if you decide that "the proper study of mankind is man" and join the increasing number of people

who find the study of astrology both rewarding and endlessly fascinating.

Astrology as a career

If you have enjoyed reading this book, you might be interested in becoming a fully-qualified practicing astrologer. There is an increasing demand for the services of consultant astrologers, in relation to which there are comparatively few fully-qualified people in practice. These are not fortune-tellers; they are people able to help others with problems by enabling them to understand themselves and others. Modern astrology is a form of psychoanalysis.

Training may involve several years of part-time study. Those wishing to take courses as a means of becoming consultants need the following qualities:

1. An interest in, and sympathy with, human nature; compassion.

2. An ability to express themselves in speech or in writing in good, clear English.

3. Integrity and a balanced philosophical outlook.

4. A sense of responsibility.

It is possible to make a living in this field, but it is very demanding work. Most consultants start on a part-time basis until they have gained experience and enlarged their clientele through personal recommendation. When they become really good, they can command high fees. However, it is not a profession in which one can become rich; it is more of a vocation, similar to that of nursing, where the main reward lies in the satisfaction of giving aid to those in need. A wide experience of life makes the best foundation.

Anyone considering this subject as a career should have a good level of all-around education. They would be advised to take a course in typing and in English and Social Studies. Some knowledge of psychology would be an asset. They would need to have a job, or some other means of support, while training and for a period of time following qualification.

There are also opportunities for those who have had training or experience in teaching. Requests for classes are growing all the time. The more mature student with skills in related fields is particularly welcome. Astrology is the study of life and is also a lifetime study that does not end with the passing of an examination.

The comparative sizes of the planets

Astronomy for the astrologer

The Solar System

		Rotation period	Year length	Diameter (M)	1000s mi from Sun
1	Sun	–	–	859.000	–
2	Mercury	59 days	88.0 days	3.000	36.000
3	Venus	249 days	224.7 days	7.600	67.000
4	Moon (Earth's)		29.5 days	2.100	93.000
5	Earth	23.9 hours	365.3 days	7.800	93.000
6	Mars	24.6 hours	687.0 days	4.200	142.000
7	Jupiter	9.8 hours	11.9 years	88.000	484.000
8	Saturn	10.2 hours	29.5 years	75.000	887.000
9	Uranus	10.8 hours	84.0 years	30.000	1.785.000
10	Neptune	15 hours	168.8 years	28.000	2.800.000
11	Pluto	6.4 days	248.4 years	3.500	3.700.000

The orbits of the planets

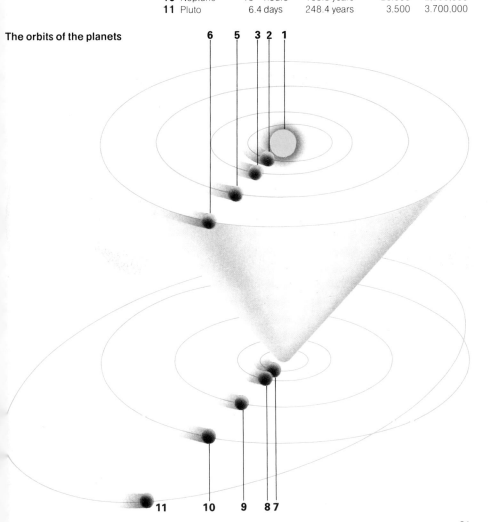

Although it is possible to set up a birthchart by rule of thumb, it is much more satisfying to know why the various calculations are made. Trained astrologers would not consider themselves fully competent if they did not understand the basic astronomy that underlies their work.

The solar system

For the purposes of astrology, we need to understand the planetary system, or the solar system as it is often called, that contains our own planet, Earth.

Our sun is the focal point of this system, which consists of nine planets circling around it in regular orbits that are not perfect ellipses.

In terms of the vast distances of the universe, Mercury, Venus, Earth, and Mars are all bunched tightly together and thus move round the sun comparatively quickly. Then comes a gap before we get to the outer planets. Jupiter, Saturn, Uranus, Neptune, and Pluto, which take considerably longer.

Jupiter takes twelve earth years to go around the sun: consequently, it is in the same sign of the zodiac for a whole year, while Saturn is in the same sign for 2½ years. The planets Uranus, Neptune, and Pluto are out at still vaster distances and are in the same zodiacal sign for seven, fourteen, and nearly twenty-one years, respectively. This explains why we say that these planets have a generation influence, rather than a personal one, in many birthcharts.

The earth and the sun

Besides making an orbit around the sun, the earth also spins around on its own axis, as if it were on a pivot fixed through its center to the North and South poles. This axis is tipped at an angle of 23½° to the earth's orbit around the sun — just as though it were a spinning top that was beginning to lose its equilibrium and sway toward the plane on which it was being rotated. This means that the amount of sunlight we receive is variable; thus, we have the seasons.

For the astronomer, the two different motions of the earth — one spinning on its own axis and completing its rotation in one day and one revolving around the sun in approximately one year — lead to complications in the measurements of both space and time.

1. **Earth's axis**
2. **Axis tipped 23½°**
3. **Sun**
4. **Rotation 23 hrs 56 mins (approx.)**

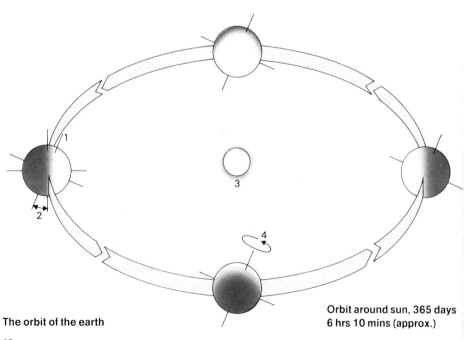

Orbit around sun, 365 days 6 hrs 10 mins (approx.)

The orbit of the earth

The Celestial Sphere

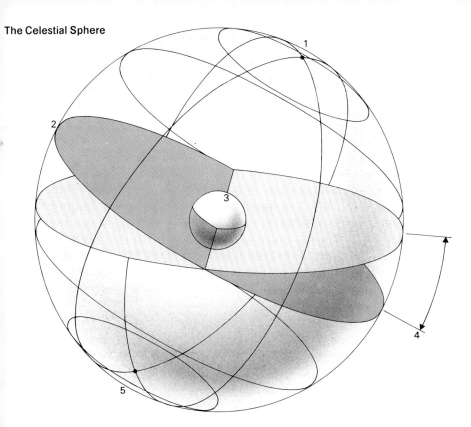

Plotting stars and planets

To be able to plot the position of a star or a planet, we need to have measurements that correspond to terrestrial latitude and longitude.

If we imagine our known universe as a great globe, with the earth as a small globe at the center of it, we are able to visualize a celestial latitude and longitude. The extension of the earth's equator to the heavens is called the *celestial equator*, and the apparent path of the sun is called the *ecliptic*.

The ecliptic and the celestial equator intersect at the vernal (or spring) equinox and at the autumnal equinox. The intersection at the vernal equinox is 0 degrees Aries (first point

of Aries) and is the point of reference that has been adopted in order to be able to plot the position of a planet or a star.

From this point, an astronomer measures in degrees, minutes, and seconds along the celestial equator in terms of right ascension – this corresponds to terrestial longitude. It is measured eastward along the celestial equator, i.e., in one direction for 360° (unlike terrestrial longitude measured from the Greenwich meridian east or west for 180°). The exact position is then fixed by measuring from the celestial equator north or south in degrees, minutes, and seconds, which is called *declination*. (There are 60 seconds in one minute and 60 minutes in 1

degree: 60"=1', 60'=1°.)

As the earth completes a rotation on its own axis in 24 hours, it turns through 360 degrees in this time, or at the rate of 1° every 4 minutes of time. (This explains the reason for adjusting by 4 minutes for each degree to find local sidereal time from Greenwich sidereal time.)

1. N Celestial Pole
2. Plane of Earth's Equator
3. Earth
4. Ecliptic 23½° from 2
5. S Celestial Pole

Measuring declination

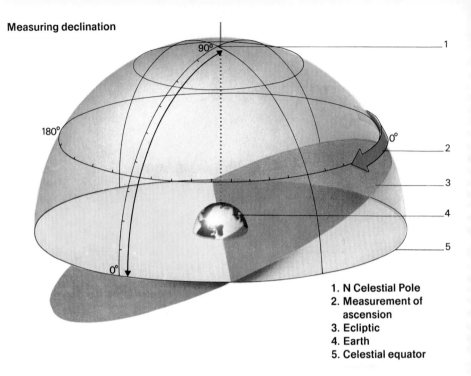

1. N Celestial Pole
2. Measurement of ascension
3. Ecliptic
4. Earth
5. Celestial equator

The zodiac

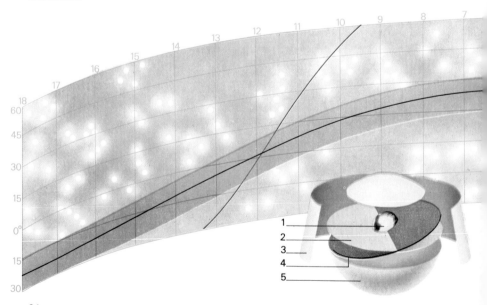

Plotting for the astrologer

The astrologer is concerned with the positions of the planets as they appear from Earth. He sees the planets against the background of the zodiac, which is to say the ecliptic, or the sun's apparent path through the heavens, widened to a band of about 8 degrees on either side. As the planets are circling round the sun, they all appear against this background (with the exception of Pluto, which can be as much as 17 degrees from the ecliptic but still following its path).

The astrologer still uses the first point of Aries as the starting place, but must measure along the ecliptic, not the equator. *Celestial longitude* is the name used for measurement eastward along the ecliptic, i.e., in the same direction as right ascension but along the ecliptic instead of the equator.

In the same way, *celestial latitude* is measured north or south of the ecliptic – in contrast to declination, which is measured north or south of the equator.

Acceleration on the interval

The earth moves around the sun at a variable speed; 24 hours is the average, or mean, solar day, since it would be impractical to adjust in terms of only seconds of time. However the earth's movement on its own axis takes approximately 23 hours and 56 minutes, so that in each 24 hours the earth has completed a revolution and is nearly 4 minutes into its next revolution. This is checked by observing the position of the stars, which appear in the same position 4 minutes earlier each night.

Thus we have a sidereal day that is 23 hours 56 minutes and a few seconds in length. Astronomers measure the sidereal day from the first point of Aries. Consequently, at the vernal equinox (March 21/22) the sidereal time will be 0 degrees 0 minutes 0 seconds. 24 hours later it will 0 degrees and nearly 4 minutes. The increase of approximately 4 minutes for each day means that we must take an adjustment for part of the day in computing a birthchart, 4 minutes in 24 hours is equal to 10 seconds per hour. This adjustment is called either *acceleration* or the *acceleration on the interval*.

1. **Earth**
2. **Celestial equator**
3. **Visible sky**
4. **Ecliptic**
5. **Celestial sphere**
6. **Zodiac**

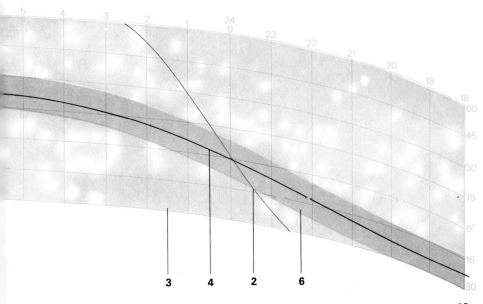

The ascendant

If we stand facing the sun at midday we will have the eastern horizon on our left, the western horizon on our right, and the south immediately in front of us. This is the way birthcharts are drawn – that is, from the point of view of the observer at the place where the native was born, so that the east point of the horizon is shown at the left of the chart and the south at the top.

Some time during the sidereal day, depending on our position, the sun is going to appear on our eastern horizon, rise to the highest point in the southern sky, then decline and set in the west. The *civil day* starts when the sun crosses the meridian point directly under the feet of the observer at midnight, local time.

This means that when the sidereal time at Greenwich is 12 noon, sidereal times in other parts of the world will vary widely according to their geographical position. As the ascendant is the point of the ecliptic rising on the eastern horizon at the time and place of birth, so this will vary widely as to both time and place and can be, literally, any sign and degree of the zodiac.

It is also necessary to remember that, although sidereal time is shown in the ephemeris as being roughly 4 minutes farther advanced each day, a complete revolution of the earth's axis has already taken place; therefore, every degree of the zodiac has passed the eastern horizon at some point during the day. It should be pointed out that the ascendant is due east only at the equinoxes; but it is convenient to chart it as if it remained due east all the time.

The Houses

As the earth rotates, the degree of the ecliptic rising changes continually, the 30 degrees of each zodiacal sign taking an average of 2 hours to pass the point of the eastern horizon, depending on the latitude. Thus if 0 degrees Aries rises at 6 a.m. at the equator, it will be followed at 8 a.m. by 0 degrees Taurus. At the point when 0 degrees Aries is rising, 0 degrees Taurus will form the cusp of the second house. It is only at the equator that all the signs rise uniformly at two hourly intervals.

As the day goes on, each sign in turn will appear on the

Movement of the Houses

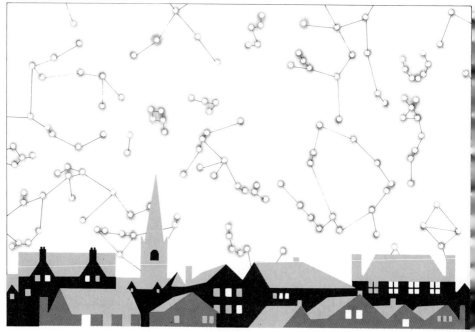

eastern horizon, rise to become the sign on the tenth house (having passed through twelfth and eleventh houses), and so on, right around the full circle of houses.

The equal house system, as used in this book,can be used for any place in the world. However, there are other house systems in general use, the most popular being Placidus, fo which the positions are given in *Raphael's Ephemeris*. Although many astrologers claim to use it with success, it is not practical for higher latitudes, as some degrees neither rise nor set in the polar regions.

Most of the systems (including Placidus) are based on the quadrant system, which gives the ascendant as the cusp of the first house and the midheaven (MC) as the cusp of the tenth house.

The other quarters of the circle

follow this pattern. The various inventors of house systems (Morinus, Campanus, Ragiomontanus, and others) all used various methods to obtain the house cusps of the intermediate houses, i.e., the ones between the quadrants.

However, it is only at the equator and at the equinoxes that the MC is actually 90 degrees away from the ascendant; and in the polar regions, some zodiacal signs do not rise at all.

Houses set up by Placidus' system are of unequal degrees and sometimes contain the whole of one zodiacal sign plus the end of the preceding one and the beginning of the following one. The whole sign, which does not appear on the cusp of any house, is then said to be "intercepted." Astrologers are not agreed as to whether this makes its influence stronger

or weaker. Interested readers are referred to further astrological textbooks for discussion of the various house systems.

NB: Much has been excluded that would appear in an ordinary astronomical textbook to avoid confusing the beginner with too much detail.

▼ Movement of the houses

The diagrams below show the apparent movement of the heavens as the earth revolves, associated with the progression of the houses.

The left-hand diagram shows the constellations above the horizon at an earlier time than in the right-hand diagram, where their position has moved higher above the horizon.

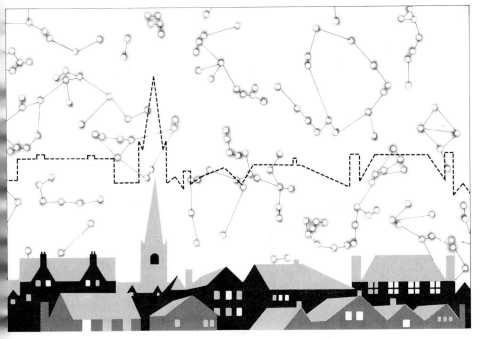

World time chart

The countries listed below are East of Greenwich and therefore the time given in hours and minutes should be added to GMT to give local time or subtracted from local time to give GMT. Further information can be found in the Nautical Almanac. (S) indicates that Daylight Savings may be kept.

	h. m.
Albania (S)	01
Algeria	01
Angola	01
Australia: Capital	
Territory	10
New South Wales	10
Northern Territory	09 30
Queensland	10
South Australia	09 30
Victoria	10
Western Australia	08
Austria	01
Bahrain	04
Belgium	01
Botswana	02
Bulgaria	02
Burma	06 30
China	08
Congo Republic W	01
E	02
Crete	02
Cyprus	02
Denmark	01
Egypt (S)	02
Finland	02
France (S)	01
German Fed. Rep.	01
Gibraltar	01
Greece	02
Hong Kong (S)	08
Hungary	01
India	05 30
Iran	03 30

Iraq	03
Israel	02
Italy (S)	01
Japan	09
Jordan	02
Kenya	03
Lebanon	02
Luxembourg	01
Malagassy Rep.	03
Malaya, Fed. of	07 30
Malta (S)	01
Mozambique	02
Netherlands	01
New Zealand	12
Nigeria	01
Norway (S)	01
Oman	04
Pakistan	05
Poland (S)	01
Rhodesia	02
Rumania	02
Singapore	07 30
South Africa	02
Sri Lanka	05 30
Sudan, Rep. of	02
Sweden	01
Switzerland	01
Syria (S)	02
Tanzania	03
Tunisia	01
Turkey	02
Uganda	03
USSR W of 40°E	02
40°E to 52°E	03
52°E to 67½°E	04
67½°E to 82½°E	05
82½°E to 87½°E	06
87½°E to 112½°E	07
112½°E to 127½°E	08
127½°E to 142½°E	09
142½°E to 157½°E	10
157½°E to 172½°E	11
E of 172½°E	12
Yugoslavia	01

Countries normally keeping GMT

Gambia	Portugal (S)
Ghana	Sierra Leone
Ireland	UK

Countries west of Greenwich, time given should be subtracted from GMT to give local time or added to local time to give GMT.

	h.
Bahamas	05
Brazil E	03
Central	04
W	05
Canada: Alberta (S)	07
British Columbia (S)	08
Manitoba (S)	06
Northwest	
Territories (S)	04 − 08
Ontario (S)	
E of 90°W	05
W of 90°W	06
Quebec (S)	
E of 60°W	04
W of 60°W	05
Saskatchewan (S)	
SE	06
remainder	07
Yukon	09
Chile	04
Ecuador	05
Haiti	05
Madeira (S)	01
Mexico (some vars.)	06
Panama	05
Paraguay	04
Peru	05
Uruguay (S)	03
USA:	
Alabama	06
Alaska	08 − 11
Arizona	07

Arkansas	06	Washington	08
California	08	West Virginia	05
Connecticut	05	Wisconsin	06
Delaware	05	Wyoming	07
Florida	05 – 06		
Georgia	05		
Hawaii	10		
Idaho	07		
Illinois	06		
Indiana	05 – 06		
Iowa	06		
Kansas	06		

Daylight Savings Time is used in many parts of the USA. During World War II, from 2nd February, 1942 to 30th September, 1945, all time zones in the U.S. advanced one hour.

The above listings are by no means exhaustive. To list all possible time variations would be a lengthy task. They do, however, indicate the considerable changes which may be encountered.

These lists relate to time zones and actual calculation of precise time differences from GMT should be made on the basis of every 15° East or West of Greenwich equalling one hour in advance or behind, respectively. Thus every degree will make a difference of four minutes.

Kentucky	06
Louisiana	06
Maine	05
Maryland	05
Massachusetts	05
Michigan	05
Minnesota	06
Mississippi	06
Missouri	06
Montana	07
Nebraska E	06
W	07
Nevada	08
New Hampshire	05
New Jersey	05
New Mexico	07
New York	05
North Carolina	05
North Dakota	06
Ohio	05
Oklahoma	06
Pennsylvania	05
Rhode Island	05
South Carolina	05
South Dakota E	06
W	07
Tennessee	06
Texas	06
Utah	07
Vermont	05
Virginia	05
Washington D.C.	05

Book list

New books on astrology are being published frequently at the present time. Some of them are valuable, but others often appear to have been written by people who give the impression of simply having read up on their subject without knowing anything about practicing it. We feel the books in this list are among the best available.

GENERAL

As above, So below,
Alan Oken, Bantam Books.

Astrologer's Handbook,
Frances Sakoian and Louis S. Acker, Harper and Row.

Astrology, the Celestial Mirror
Warren Kenton, Avon.

Astrological Chart of the U.S. from 1776 to 2141,
Gar Osten, Stein and Day.

The Astrological Houses,
Dave Rudhyar, Penguin.

Astrology,
Christopher McIntosh, Harper and Row.

Astrology,
Louis MacNeice, Doubleday.

Astrology and Religion Among the Greeks and Romans,
Franz Cumont, Dover.

Astrology: Evolution and Revolution,
Alan Oken, Bantam Books.

Astrology for Adults,
Joan Quigley, Warner Books.

Astrology: How and Why It Works,
Marc E. Jones, Penguin.

Astrology of Human Relationships,
Frances Sakoian and Louis S. Acker, Harper and Row.

Astrology of Relationships,
Michael Meyer, Doubleday.

Astrology: Sense or Nonsense?
Roy A. Gallant, Doubleday.

Astrology Terms,
Leslie Fleming-Mitchell, Running Press.

The Case for Astrology,
John West and Jan G. Toonder, Coward, McCann.

The Compleat Astrologer,
Derek & Julie Parker, McGraw-Hill.

The Cosmic Clocks,
Michael Gauquelin, Contemporary Books.

From Pioneer to Poet,
Isabelle M. Pagan, Theosophical Publishing House.

The Practice of Astrology,
Dane Rudhyar, Penguin.

Sun Sign Rising,
Maria E. Grummere, Ballantine.

The Zodiac and the Soul,
C.E.O. Carter, Theosophical Publishing House.

ASTRONOMY

Astronomy,
Frank N. Bash, Harper and Row.

Astronomy,
D.S. Evans, McKay.

Astronomy, a Brief Introduction,
Walter H. Hesse, Addison-Wesley.

Astronomy: A Popular History,
Johann Dorschner, Van Nostrand.

Astronomy for Everyman,
Martin Davidson, Dutton.

Astronomy for the Amateur,
John Gribbin, McKay.

Astronomy: How Man Learned About the Universe,
L.W. Page, Addison-Wesley.

Astronomy Made Simple,
(revised edition), Meir H. Degani, Doubleday.

Astronomy of the Twentieth Century,
Otto Struve and Velta Zebergs, Macmillan.

Glossary

Acceleration on the Interval: the adjustment made to allow for a sidereal day being shorter than a civil day.

Air: the name of one of the Triplicities (or elements). The zodiacal signs are Gemini, Libra and Aquarius.

Aries: first sign of the zodiac. The sun is in this sign from March 21 to April 19.

Ascendant: the sign and degree of the zodiac that is rising on the eastern horizon at the time and place of birth. It also forms the cusp of the first house of the birthchart and is the first point which is plotted onto the birthchart.

Aquarius: eleventh sign of the zodiac. The sun is in this sign from January 20 to February 18.

Aspect: planets are said to be in aspect if they are in certain relationships to each other.

Birthchart: or "horoscope". A chart of the positions of the sun, moon and planets at a given moment of time as seen from a precise spot on the earth. It can be set up, "erected" or "cast", to represent the planetary positions at the birth time of any person, project or event.

Bundle: a chart shaping in which all the planets are within 120 degrees (a trine).

Cancer: fourth sign of the zodiac. The sun is in this sign from June 22 to July 22.

Capricorn: tenth sign of the zodiac. The sun is in this sign from December 22 to January 19.

Cardinal: the name given to one of the Quadruplicities (or qualities). The zodiacal signs Aries, Cancer, Libra and Capricorn are Cardinal Signs.

Civil Day: the 24 hour mean solar day.

Common signs: another name for mutable signs.

Conjunction: the aspect when two planets are within 8° of each other.

Constellations: astronomically accepted groupings of stars. The ones on the ecliptic have given their names to the zodiacal signs, although they do not coincide.

Cusp: name given to the line that divides two zodiacal signs or two houses.

Descendant: the degree of the zodiac which is setting at the western horizon at the time and place of birth.

Ecliptic: the apparent path of the sun through the heavens.

Earth: the name of one of the Triplicities (or elements). The zodiacal signs of Taurus, Virgo and Capricorn are earth signs.

Electional astrology: a method used to choose a birth time for a project which is in the future.

Elements, The: Fire, earth, air and water, which each consist of three of the zodiacal signs.

Fire: the name of one of the Triplicities (or elements). The zodiacal signs of Aries, Leo and Sagittarius are fire signs.

Fixed: The name given to one of the Quadruplicities (or qualities). The zodiacal signs of Taurus, Leo, Scorpio and Aquarius are fixed signs.

Gemini: third sign of the zodiac. The sun is in this sign from May 21 to June 21.

Generation influence: the outer planets remain in the same zodiacal sign for long periods, and thus "influence" a whole generation.

Glyph: the sign used for a planet or zodiacal name. Astrological "shorthand".

Grand Cross: a pattern formed

by two oppositions at right angles to each other.

Grand Trine: a pattern formed by three planets in trine aspect to eath other.

Greenwich Meridian: the line at Greenwich Observatory from which degrees of longitude are determined eastward and westward. It represents 0° Longitude.

Houses: divisions of the birthchart numbered from the ascendant in a counterclockwise direction.

Imum Coeli: IC, the opposite point on the birthchart to the midheaven (MC).

Keywords: a memory aid devised by Mrs. Margaret Hone to describe each of the planets and zodiacal signs.

Leo: fifth sign of the zodiac. The sun is in this sign from July 23 to August 22.

Libra: seventh sign of the zodiac. The sun is in this sign from September 23 to October 23.

Lights, The: a phrase used to denote the sun and moon together.

MC: (Medium coeli), the point immediately overhead at the time and place of birth.

Midheaven: see MC.

Mundane astrology: the type of astrology that studies political and economic trends.

Mutable: the name given to one of the Quadruplicities (or qualities). The zodiacal signs of Gemini, Virgo, Sagittarius and Pisces are mutable signs.

Mutual reception: the relationship between two planets when each falls in the zodiacal sign ruled by the other.

Negative signs: signs in the Earth or Water Triplicities are negative.

Opposition: the aspect when two planets are opposite each other, i.e. at 180°

Pisces: twelfth sign of the zodiac. The sun is in this sign from February 19 to March 20.

Polarity: a sign of the zodiac is said to be in polarity with its opposite sign.

Positive signs: signs with fire and air triplicities are positive.

Quadruplicities: the Cardinal, Fixed and Mutable qualities. Four of the zodiacal signs come into each group.

Rising planet: see Strong planet.

Sagittarius: ninth sign of the

zodiac. The sun is in this sign from November 22 to December 21.

Scorpio: eighth sign of the zodiac. The sun is in this sign from October 24 to November 21.

Seesaw: a chart shaping where the planets fall into two groups in opposition.

Sextile: the aspect when the planets are 60 degrees apart.

Shaping: the pattern made by the grouping of the planets on the birthchart, often taken into account in interpretation.

Sidereal time: star time.

Splash: a chart shaping in which planets are spread over a wide area of the chart.

Square: the aspect when the planets are 90 degrees apart.

"Strong" planet: any planet within 8° of the Ascendant (also called a "rising planet) or any planet in its "own" sign. Carries more "weight" in an interpretation than planets not so placed.

Synastry: the comparison of two or more birthcharts.

Taurus: second sign of the zodiac. The sun is in this sign from April 20 to May 20.

Index

Trine: the aspect when the planets are 120 degrees apart from each other.

Triplicities: see Elements.

T-Square: the pattern formed by an opposition aspect between two planets with a third planet square to both of them.

Virgo: sixth sign of the zodiac. The sun is in this sign from August 23 to September 22.

Water: the name of one of the Triplicities (or elements). The zodiacal signs of Cancer, Scorpio and Pisces are water signs.

Zodiac: the background of the sky 8° on either side of the ecliptic. For astrological purposes this is divided into twelve equal sections of thirty degrees. Each section has the name of a sign of the Zodiac.

Credits

Artists
Ron Hayward Associates
John Shackell

Photographs
Aerofilms: 15
Archives Photographiques Paris: 51
Data Section Astrological Association: 7, 54, 55, 68
Bodleian Library: 35, 45

Californian Historical Society: 23
Peter Clayton: 14
Ray Gardner: 47
Sonia Halliday: 19, 29, 33
Mary Evans Picture Library: 6, 28, 40, 42, 46, 49, 50
Michael Holford: 5, 30
Mansell Collection: contents. 6, 32, 34, 37, 38, 43, 44
National Maritime Museum: 11, 59

Orlandini/Bib. Estense: 20
Photic: 22
Photomas: 24, 35, 65
Popperfoto: 12, 16
Radio Times Hulton Picture Library: 6, 39, 43, 54, 55
Ronan Picture Library: contents, 17, 21
Royal Astronomical Society: contents
SEF: 61
Victoria & Albert Museum: 48